On the
Trout Stream
with
Joe Humphreys

On the Trout Stream with Joe Humphreys

Photographs by Boyd Pfeiffer

Illustrations by George Lavanish

STACKPOLE
BOOKS

Published by
STACKPOLE BOOKS
Cameron and Kelker Streets
P.O. Box 1831
Harrisburg, PA 17105

Printed in the United States of America

10 9 8 7 6 5 4 3 2 1

First edition

Library of Congress Cataloging-in-Publication Data

Humphreys, Joseph B., 1929–
    On the trout stream with Joe Humphreys / photographs by Boyd
Pfeiffer ; illustrations by George Lavanish.—1st ed.
        p.   cm.
    ISBN 0-8117-1156-0
    1. Fly fishing. 2. Trout fishing. I. Title.
SH451.H795   1989
    799.1'755—dc20   89-33191
                                                      CIP

Dedication

With fond memories
of my parents, Ruth and James M. Humphreys,
and my brother Richard

With thanks
to my sisters, Helen and Mardy,
and to my wife, Gloria,
and daughters, Johanna and Dolores

With gratitude
to my mentor and friend
George Harvey
for his patience, wisdom, guidance,
and understanding

Contents

Acknowledgments

The author thanks the following people for their help in putting this book together:

Photographers Boyd Pfeiffer, Kathy Holesworth, Martha Holt, Tom Greenlee, and Paul Blankenhorn

George Lavanish for his photography and line drawings

Fishing students Cindy Miller and my nephew Todd Biddle

WE WANTED TO MAKE A BOOK OF FLY-FISHING INSTRUCTION THAT would approximate a series of real-life, on-the-stream lessons with a master.

Assuming that outdoor sports are taught better outdoors than at a typewriter, we waded the trout waters of northern Pennsylvania with a camera and a tape recorder beside Joe Humphreys as he addressed his prodigious talents to a host of stream challenges. Then—under Joe's supervision—came the onerous task of refining a rather intimidating mass of raw material down into the volume you hold in your hands.

It's a different book, something of an experiment, informal, visual, conversational, repetitive (like any lesson), emotional at times, a book, we feel, to be browsed through as well as read page by page, a book to be lingered over.

There's a lot about fly fishing that some of us who feel we've progressed beyond the beginner stage think we understand. But when you start learning the basics of fly fishing as Joe Humphreys teaches them, two things happen. First, fishing suddenly becomes more complicated, harder work. Secondly, you discover you're catching more fish and having more fun!

Joe's energy on the stream is wondrous. He's continually positioning, adjusting, experimenting, analyzing, moving on to new water, trying again, always trying. The only thing it's sure Joe Humphreys will never learn about fly fishing is how to give up. It's exhausting, following him, and there's a lesson to be learned when you see Joe persist and take trout where you knew—you *knew*—there'd be no action.

Maybe, you think to yourself, all the trouble this guy goes to, all the pains he takes, all the pondering and figuring he does, all the complicated and subtle variations he builds into his casts and the long, fish-less moments he will devote to reconstructing his entire leader simply in preparation for a single run or pool, is worth it—this guy knows what he's talking about!

Joe's teaching isn't always what we're accustomed to hearing set forth as generally accepted fly-fishing procedure. This isn't because he's unorthodox—it's because most of the time he's gone deeper, in his on-the-stream analysis and experimentation, than anyone else. Often he's ahead of his time. Eight years ago, when Joe said in TROUT TACTICS that you nymph with your rod tip elevated, more than one reviewer took him to task—today the elevated rod tip is universally accepted.

The short—"*tap*"—casting stroke. Changing levels. Presenting the dry fly at an angle. Adjustment of nymphs/weights/tippet for extended bottom roll. Fishing the velocity change. S-curves in the dryfly leader. The role of the third and fourth fingers of the casting hand . . . any one of these basics would merit a full summer's attention, and, in that sense, ON THE TROUT STREAM is a book to be read and absorbed gradually.

Pondered, practiced—practiced some more, each basic starts to take on a depth of meaning and feel in the angler's muscle-memory. We can't hope to become super-expert like Joe—it would be exhausting even to try. But we can teach ourselves *some* of his techniques, make them habit—second-nature when we venture out onto the stream. Then, suddenly, we find we're catching more fish; we're catching bigger fish. Most fun of all we're starting to take trout in those difficult stream situations where previously we would've gotten skunked for certain.

There's more: Joe's favorite ties, a surefire nymphing trick, leader/tippet specs, knots, striking-playing-landing, casts for small streams, night-nymphing advice, how to read temperature and conditioning . . .

In conversation with you, the reader, Joe tells and shows how to catch trout on a fly, teaches you, in a depth of detail we feel is unprecedented, what he knows . . . ON THE TROUT STREAM is a full book. We hope you enjoy it. We hope you learn half as much from reading it as we learned from putting it together.

The action takes place on public water and is authentic. Any inconsistencies—inaccuracies—are solely the fault of the editors. The knowledge, wisdom, and fishing joy are pure Joe Humphreys.

The Editors

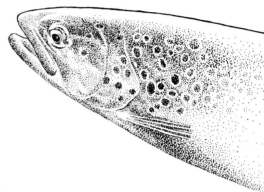

Introduction

I HAVE ALWAYS FELT THAT INTRODUCTIONS SHOULD BE SHORT AND TO the point, and I'm getting too old to start changing now.

Naturally I'm flattered that someone with the status of Joe Humphreys would ask me to introduce his latest literary effort.

It has been better than fifteen years since we first teamed up as fly-fishing instructors. During that time I have become firmly convinced that I was watching one of the rare masters of the art of fly fishing. It is certainly a pleasure to stand back and observe and, yes, admire the preciseness with which Joe consistently demonstrates his casting and fishing expertise for his students. The same expertise is passed on to you throughout this latest collection of instructions from one who has gathered and mastered the techniques over a period of more than fifty years.

Many of the techniques are original with Joe and not someone else's ideas that he is trying to pawn off as his own. One of the many things that impresses me about Joe, above and beyond the fact that he is a first-rate caster and angler, is the fact that he does not hesitate to give credit to others if this credit is deserved.

So this is my introduction to Joe and his latest book. You'd better pay attention lest you miss some topnotch information from a world-class fisherman, instructor, and friend.

Ed Shenk

Nymphing

AS YOU MOVE ALONG THE STREAM FISHING NYMPHS YOU'RE GOING to encounter varying velocities of water, varying clarity of water, varying depths. The key is to adjust. Stop fishing and take the time to put another weight on, or to take one off, or to slightly adjust the position of your weights, or to change the diameter of that tippet, or to put on a heavier or lighter nymph. You do this in response to the water you're facing, to get the exact rig that's going to roll your nymph along naturally down on the streambottom where you want it. I carry my split-shot loose in a pocket so I can take a handful out and analyze the water I'm going to be working and pick out the exact weight-size or sizes I want.

It's work. This kind of fishing can drive people crazy. They don't see the necessity, or if they do they don't want to take all that time and trouble to be constantly fiddling with their weights. But why fish with something that doesn't work? If your nymphs are drifting along three feet off the bottom or if they're shooting through that pocket water too fast, what good is it?

With the proper weight adjustment we have a better shot. We give our nymph a little more time down there, a longer bottom roll. You don't need much change. Half the time it's just a matter of moving your weights into a different position relative to your flies—pull them down closer to that point nymph if you want to get deeper, pull them up, a little further away, if you've got shallower water coming up.

Make the change. Read the water, then make damned sure your rig is set up to get your flies down where you want them with that good, natural roll along the bottom.

I'm starting off with a weighted nymph for my point fly *(see facing page),* some split-shot, because I figure I'll need that little bit of weight to get down into the particular pocket of water I'm looking at, then a lighter-weight nymph for my top fly, because I want that one to ride higher than the first one. My nymphs are color-coded as to weight—brown head for middle-weight, yellow for light-weight, black for heavy—so I know at a glance what weight nymph I'm putting where. I'm leaving my two pieces of split-shot eight to ten inches above my point nymph, which should give it a deeper ride. And notice my weights aren't slammed together. I have some space between them, which gives a more even roll along the bottom.

A pair of *Isonychia* mayfly nymphs—these really produce. Look how much movement I've tied into that one on the lower right. Soft emu feathers for the gills. Fur for the body, soft hen hackles for the legs, soft tail fibers . . . that critter's going to *pulsate* as it rolls over the bottom.

BEFORE YOU START FISHING THAT NYMPH, ROUGH IT UP. RUB IT ON A rock. This does three things. It gives the fly a more natural look. It roughens the shape, kicks some guard hairs out, which means more movement when it's down there bouncing and rolling along the bottom, and it takes my smell off and puts a natural smell on.

Trout can smell. I don't want my smell on that fly. They can very easily back off. The food chain gives off a definite scent and the trout are familiar with it. The whole thing's sight, smell, shape, movement, and color, the total picture of what that trout's conditioned to, what's carried along to him by the current—you want to try and put all the pieces of the puzzle together.

Barbless hooks are in, and they should be. I'll pinch that barb down before I fish. But that doesn't mean you shouldn't sharpen up your hook. Take a little stone or some other sharpening material and get a good sharp point on that hook before you fish it.

4

The Tuck Cast

Here's the Tuck Cast, the basic nymphing cast, in brief. First, lift as much line off the water as you can.

Start the line moving and kick the wrist up with the thumb pointing up and . . .

. . . *tap* it. Stop the rod. Your line begins to straighten out behind you.

You're starting to drift your rod forward as your line continues to straighten out behind you. You're waiting to feel the tug when the weighted nymph pulls on your line. When you feel the tug of the weighted nymph as the line straightens out behind you . . .

. . . start the forward stroke and . . .

. . . *tap.* Stop your rod sharply. Check it. The last two fingers of your casting hand pull *back* as the thumb pushes forward then imperceptibly bounces back and up.

The impulse travels out through

your extending line

forward and down, tucking your weighted nymph into the water.

7

THE IDEA IS TO CAST MY NYMPHS UP TO THE HEAD OF THE RUN OR pocket, casting them in such a way as to get them down to the bottom of the stream as quickly as possible once they've hit the water. This way I immediately get that good natural bottom-roll that means I'm maximizing my chances as my flies drift downstream over the bottom toward me. Once they're rolling back downstream over the bottom toward me I want to keep in touch—keep all excess slack out of my line—and this is done by keeping my rod tip up, steadily retrieving line, slowly elevating my rod tip as the drift comes toward me over the bottom.

The top photo to the right shows the beginning of the cast. I've lifted as much line as I can off the water. Now I get the line moving, using my hand, wrist, and forearm. I'm concentrating—throughout the entire cast—on the spot I want to cast to. I *accelerate* and drift that line behind me—look how little my hand moves.

With dry flies you're casting the weight of the line, but with weighted nymphs you're casting the weight of your flies, in part, so on the backcast it's crucial to feel the tug of the weighted nymphs as you start to drift the rod forward, then make the forward stroke.

Notice I'm giving it a little haul. My hand that's holding the line is pulling down, stripping a few inches of line preparatory to shooting—releasing—that same portion of line later, in the forecast. I've calculated I'll want a bit of extra distance to get right up to the head of the run.

No cast is ever made one exact way over and over—there are variations, modifications, that you learn to make by second nature, by instinct. To the right we have an example. The computer under my hat has figured I'm going to need a few extra feet of distance and rather than falsecast out that extra line I'm going to just give it a little haul and shoot it.

Editors' Note: On the following 11 pages (through page 19), to show the all-important action of the fingers of Joe's casting hand, we drew a right hand, even though Joe, as you can see from the photos, casts lefty.

I feel the tug on the rod tip as my weighted nymphs straighten the line out behind me. I start my rod forward. I'm loading that rod, getting the inertia of those nymphs pulling back on the rod as the rod pulls—drifts—forward in the beginning of the powerstroke. My thumb's on top of the rod handle pointing toward the target and I'm using my fingers and wrist. I'm looking at my target—total concentration. Remember, you want to bring that rod straight overhead when you come through on the forecast. When you're casting weighted nymphs you want your wrist straight—vertical—when you bring your rod forward. Otherwise you can cowtail, and you'll be throwing a loop and you'll be out of touch with your nymphs. From the pickup through the backcast and forecast to the check, your hand—seen from above—makes a slight circle, or oval (as shown below) to avoid your line kicking against itself or against your rod. But coming through on the forecast and check you want that wrist straight and that rod coming through *straight* overhead.

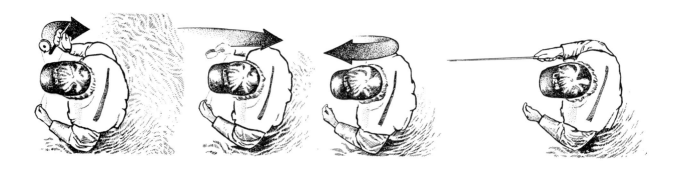

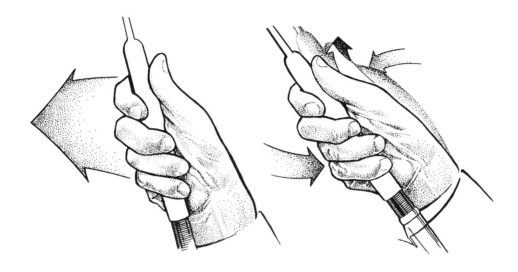

Now the check. I stop my rod decisively, sharply, with a firm forward push of the thumb and simultaneously a pulling back and up with the last two fingers of my casting hand. It's a quick squeeze—*bam*—my hand squeezes the rod handle as I do it—thumb forward, last two fingers pulling back in, toward me, *bam*, subtle, almost imperceptible, forceful and sharp.

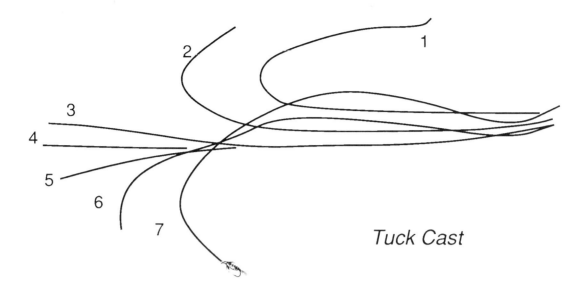

Tuck Cast

Note: The action of the last two fingers of the casting hand (see lower arrow on preceding page) is crucial. It's not just the thumb, it's also your third and fourth fingers pulling back and in at the same time the thumb pushes forward, when you sharply check the rod on the forecast. Experiment with this—get the feel of what this does to rod and line.

I check (stop the rod sharply) and pull back. My hand bounces back toward me off the check (see photo at right). It's barely perceptible. Bam: check-squeeze, thumb pushes and last two fingers pull, hand bounces back—all done in the space of an inch and in less than a second's time. Energy is directed forward and downward through the line causing my weighted nymph to tuck in at an angle and settle down through the water to the bottom where I want it. You can see I've thrown a relatively shallow tuck, meaning my line's going out at a relatively shallow angle to the water—this will bring my nymph in, when it enters the water, at a relatively shallow angle. The higher you check your rod on the tuck cast, the steeper the angle of the cast. The longer you wait before making the check—in other words the further you let your rod drift forward before checking it—the shallower the cast . . .

. . . and that's what I've done here (right). I've shot a modified tuck at a relatively gentle angle up to the head of the pocket. Notice I've released that line I had stripped out a few photos ago. This gives me the extra distance I wanted. Making that little haul also sped up the line, increasing the impetus of the tuck.

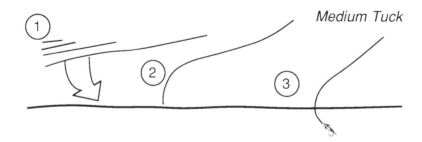

Medium Tuck

Here's a deeper tuck. Coming forward I've checked my rod a touch higher, which will steepen the angle of my line to the water, and the nymph is driving down. Bam, I popped it, pushed with the thumb and pulled with my last two fingers and my hand bounced back off the check and to sharpen the angle I made a little lift, *lifted* my casting hand, just a touch, off the check—this is all in the space of a fraction of an inch, barely perceptible, but decisive and firm—*bam* . . .

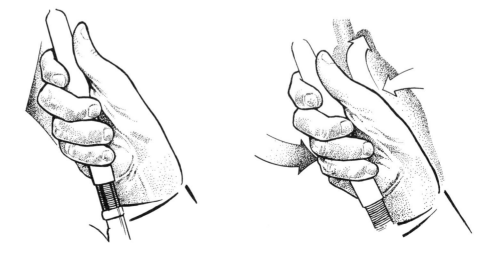

14

. . . that loop's much tighter now. Eyes on my target. Line control with my non-casting hand. That sharp, high check caused my rod to bend forward, load forward, and as it unloads . . .

Editors' Note: The above photo was spliced into this series from a different "deep-tuck-cast" sequence.

... my nymph is driven down at a steeper angle toward the water. That little loop up there at my rod tip shows just how sharply my high, lifting check is sending my nymph down toward the water. I check high and hard with a lift—bam—which causes my rod to bend forward driving and dropping my nymph down at a sharper angle to the water.

16

And as the cast concludes the deep tuck takes place and drags the nymph in at a steep angle. The end of my line collapses, or plunges downward, getting my weighted nymph down in at that steep angle I want. If the water's deeper I want an even steeper angle as my nymph enters the water so it'll get to the bottom fast and start the bottom roll as soon as possible—there might be a fish at the head of the pocket, and if I don't get my nymph to him I don't have a chance.

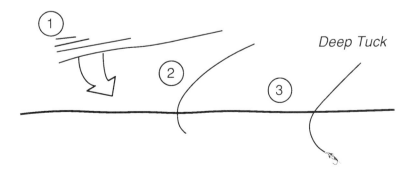

Deep Tuck

Here's a *very shallow tuck.* Look how far I've drifted my rod forward *(above)* before making the check. Remember, check it high and short and your tuck will be deep and steep, check out in front of you—let your rod drift well forward on the forecast before you check—and you'll get a shallow tuck *(see two photos at right)*. Look at how my rod bends forward when I squeeze and check. Then *(above photo to your right)* my rod bounces back up, slightly, sending the impulse of the check all the way out through the line and leader to the nymph.

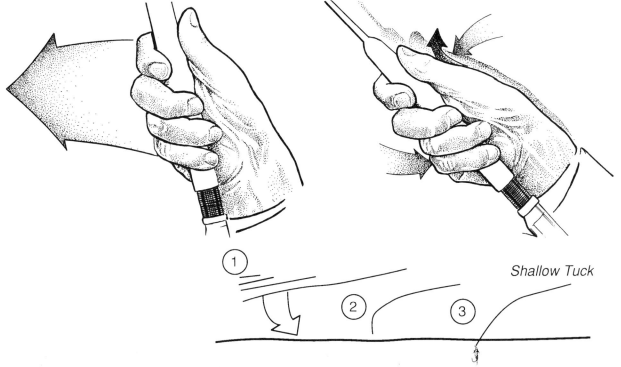

Shallow Tuck

The Downer-Upper

The Downer-Upper is a short-distance cast that drives my nymph down in at a very steep angle. I use this cast, which is really a compact version of the Tuck, for situations where I want to drive my nymphs forcefully into the very top of the pocket. Using a compact, spare motion I lift my line off the water at a *steep* angle—look at how little my casting hand has moved to achieve this. Note also how I "climb the angle," or bring my line back up behind me *(above)* through approximately the same angle my line formed with the water when I first lifted it off the water *(left)*. Again, my casting hand and wrist move very little, considering the pull I'm generating, and, as always, the rest of me is still—I'm concentrating on exactly where I want to pinpoint the cast.

My nymphs are up high behind me as I start the forward drift. My thumb and the middle row of knuckles of my casting hand point right at the target, straight forward at the spot I'm casting to.

I bring the rod *straight* forward, keeping it in the vertical plane of the cast so I don't cowtail, and here's the check—it comes quick and high—the Downer-Upper is an extremely short casting stroke: thumb checks sharply forward and down— *bam*—driving that nymph down. I've pulled my elbow in toward me and lifted with those all-important last two fingers of my casting hand. Look what my casting hand has done from the photo at left to the photo above—that's the check.

My rod is arced with the forward and downward bend that my sharp "Downer" check threw into it,

. . . sending my line, and nymph, *down*. This is a steep angle, I'm really firing my nymph down into the water I want to cover. My hand and elbow haven't moved. I've done my work, the rod's done its work, and now the weighted nymph is doing its work.

Just before my nymph goes in . . .

... I give it the "Upper," a fast little lift of my casting hand and forearm. Thumb and rod point up, as you can see. This swift move drives my nymph down in at a still sharper angle. This cast is less of a tuck in that my nymph doesn't really tuck back under the leader but instead, once I've given it the "Upper," shoots straight down in. Rod's high at the finish as I begin to fish the cast out. I have little or no line on the water and I'm in close contact with my nymph as it starts its roll along the bottom.

Cross-Chest

YOU HAVE TO LEARN TO CAST AT EVERY ANGLE, WITH A VARIETY OF different strokes—it's all just a variation on that basic lift, *tap*, drift forward, *tap*. Here I'm making the cross-chest tuck, which I might use if I had obstructions blocking me on the side where I usually cast. I take it back across my chest *(below)* and over the opposite shoulder. I lift it, *tap* it, and that weighted nymph straightens my line out behind me and I feel that slight tug *(facing page above)*. Then I start the forecast *(facing page below)*, loading the rod and . . .

. . . here's the squeeze, the forward tap, or check . . .

. . . driving that nymph down . . .

. . . at a steep angle to the water.

PRACTICE THESE CASTS. EXPERIMENT. GET THE FEEL OF THE LIFT OFF
the water, the *tap* for the backcast, the drift forward and the *tap* for the forecast.

Practice until you get the feel of these different casts in your muscles. Then
when you go out on the stream with the muscle-memory you won't tighten up
when you face a difficult casting situation. You'll be able to concentrate on the
water you're casting to and stay relaxed and loose throughout the whole motion, lift . . . *tap* . . . drift . . . *tap*.

You'll be able to program your mind with the cast you want to make and,
staying relaxed and smooth, you'll make that cast, working that all-important
thumb-and-last-two-fingers-combo to get the exact effect you want.

Think about your wrist, your wrist and your hand—your thumb and your
third and fourth fingers—that's what you do it with, occasionally using your
forearm too. It's wrist, thumb, fingers—lift, tap, drift forward and *tap* it. *Push*
with the thumb and pull—*squeeze*—back in with those last two fingers. Do it
over and over, practice the variations until they're second nature and you don't
have to think about it consciously every time you do it on the stream. Virtually
every cast, nymphs, dry flies, wet flies, is a variation on the lift, *tap* it, drift it
forward to where you want it and *tap* it, *check* it, with that subtle and firm,
imperceptible squeeze.

In Under
An Obstruction

Throwing a weighted nymph in under an obstruction, such as some tree branches *(right)*, is tough. You really use your wrist. Once you've felt the tug of the weight of the nymph straightening your line out behind you . . .

. . . you start the forecast, drifting your rod tip beyond (i.e. in your line of sight to the level of, or slightly below) the obstruction you want to get in under. Then you squeeze off the tap forward and unload all the power in the rod. Let me say that again. On the forecast you're drifting your rod tip forward and the instant your rod tip drops to the level of or below the level of the obstruction you squeeze off the check sharply, throwing the weight of your nymph . . .

. . . in under those branches.

The Rolling Tuck

I developed the Rolling Tuck for situations where I have an obstruction right behind me and no room for a backcast. It's also a great way to drive your nymphs down in at a sharp angle. You lift, as shown, drifting your line behind the rod tip, so it bellies . . .

. . . to load the rod . . .

. . . and once you have the belly you accelerate forward and give it a very sharp check with the thumb snapping forward and the last two fingers pulling back. The loop rolls forward.

Editors' Note: As in the photos above, occasionally the line has been accented by an artist, to emphasize position and direction.

As the loop straightens out you lift, as shown above. This is a level change *up*. I've abruptly lifted my rod to steepen the angle at which my nymph enters the water.

Down into the current my nymph is driven and I'll get that good natural bottom-roll almost at once. Thumb and knuckles pointing toward target. Rod high. Now let's take a look at how, once I've delivered my nymph to the water with the right cast for the situation, I fish the cast out. . . .

Once your nymph has made its entry into the water and settled to the bottom you stay in touch with it, as it drifts back to you, by slowly elevating your rod tip, watching all the time for any subtle line movement, which could signify a strike. My elbow comes back in and my rod tip lifts as the drift begins: that natural, gently rolling and bouncing motion of the nymph as it tumbles back downstream over the bottom toward me. I'm lifting my rod tip. I'm gradually stripping in line to keep that line just as tight as possible from rod tip to nymph. I'm going to continue doing this the whole way through the drift. I want my line, leader, and tippet in as straight a line as possible to my nymph as it bottom-rolls back downstream toward me.

Keeping my rod tip up, lifting that tip as my weighted nymph comes tumbling back downstream over the bottom toward me, I'm maintaining that all-important angle—between line and rod—that creates that little bit of slack that gives the fish time to suck my fly in when he hits. Call it a 90° angle—sometimes it's less, sometimes it's more. In the photos above it's a little sharper than 90°. It's that same angle—between line and rod—that you want to preserve as you fish out your cast whether you're fishing wet flies or nymphs. Yes you want to be in tight touch from rod tip to nymph, but at the same time you want that angle so you can get that little bit of slack—you can see it in my line, which is not perfectly straight—that gives the fish the couple inches of line he needs to allow him to inhale—and that's what they do.

I'm working a nice little velocity change, right where that shadow's protruding to the right of the big rock. There's a slight shelving drop-off there and a nice, subtle change in currents as a result—that's what they like, those changes in velocity. I'm lifting my rod-tip, stripping in line—if I see hesitation, if I feel the slightest bump, if I feel or see anything that seems the least bit strange, I strike. You'll hang up on the bottom a lot. If you're not hanging up now and then on those bottom rocks you're not nymphing properly—you're not getting down there for that good natural bottom-roll, you're not getting down to where the fish are.

TAKE THE TIME TO MAKE THE NECESSARY WEIGHT ADJUSTMENT FOR the water you're nymphing. I've said it before and I'll say it again: Maximizing your fishing time by keeping your nymph in productive water as long and as naturally as possible is paramount. When it's drifting at the wrong speed or at the wrong depth it isn't maximizing your fishing time. Stop. Make the adjustment.

If you've made the right cast and you're keeping that rod tip elevated and stripping in line and concentrating on a good natural drift and your nymph is coming back to you too fast—not getting down on the bottom for that natural roll, you don't have enough weight. Your nymph is going past those fish too fast. If your nymph is coming back too fast, or if you're about to move from shallower or slower water to deeper or faster water, stop and adjust to increase your weight.

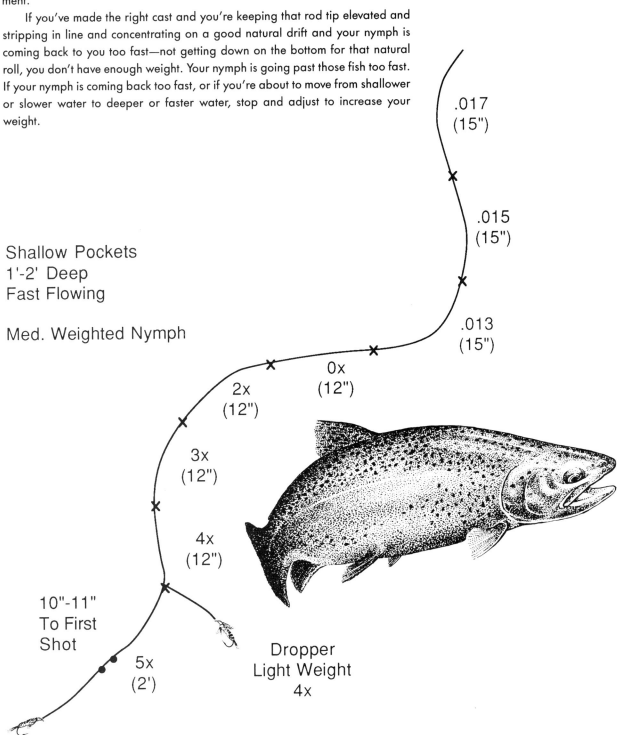

.017
(15")

.015
(15")

Shallow Pockets
1'-2' Deep
Fast Flowing

Med. Weighted Nymph

.013
(15")

0x
(12")

2x
(12")

3x
(12")

4x
(12")

10"-11"
To First
Shot

5x
(2')

Dropper
Light Weight
4x

IF YOU'RE REPEATEDLY HANGING UP OR IF YOU'RE GOING TO MOVE from a deeper or swifter stretch to water that's shallower or slower, stop and go to the trouble to decrease your weight. It could be a question of sliding the weight you already have on up, away from your point fly, or taking a weight off, or putting a lighter weight or weights on. In the extreme you might have to rebuild your leader, break off the tippet and tie a longer section on if you're going to a lighter pair of nymphs . . . but it's worth it.

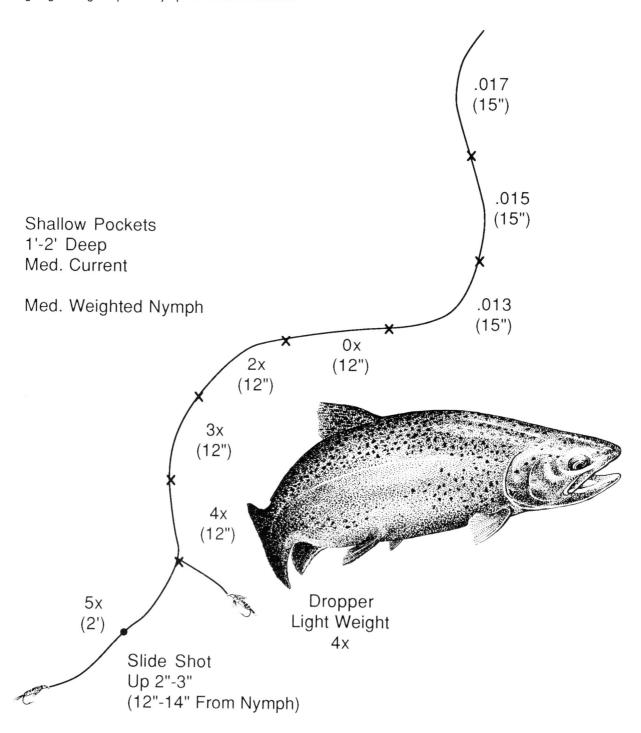

.017
(15")

.015
(15")

Shallow Pockets
1'-2' Deep
Med. Current

Med. Weighted Nymph

.013
(15")

0x
(12")

2x
(12")

3x
(12")

4x
(12")

Dropper
Light Weight
4x

5x
(2')

Slide Shot
Up 2"-3"
(12"-14" From Nymph)

Stream Situations

TO CATCH TROUT ON A NYMPH, CONSIDER THESE POINTS . . .

Fish the velocity changes. You want your nymph drifting along the imprecise border areas where a faster current meets a slower one. There are many such velocity changes, some of them quite subtle, and they're marked by changes on the surface of the stream, as well as changes in the lightness or darkness of the water.

Lift your line over as many current changes as possible. You can do this by positioning yourself to cast over the currents, but sometimes this is easier said than done. A long rod is a help—it enables you to lift over, in other words to hold your line up over, the current changes between you and the fish.

Don't let the fish see you. If that water's clear and you short-line you're decreasing your odds 50 percent. Maybe you won't see them but they'll see you. Consider your approach carefully. Keep your profile *low*. Master the tuck cast and its variations so you can shoot to the head of the pool or pocket or well out across the currents to the area you want to fish. If the water is clear you don't want to stand close to the water you're fishing. If the water's low and clear, shoot for distance. If the water's clear but broken you can get a little closer, but only a little—you still want to be casting for distance. If the water's off-color you can get closer, and if that water's off-color and broken you can get closer still.

Lead your nymph with the rod tip the whole way through the drift. Keep the rod tip ahead of the nymph as the drift proceeds downstream. If you're nymphing directly upstream this means lifting your rod tip as your fly bottom-rolls back to you . . . if you're fishing across it means keeping your rod tip downstream ahead of your nymph at all times during the drift. Keep as much slack or belly out of that line as humanly possible. You want to keep in close contact from the line in your hands right out through the rod tip and down through your line and leader to your nymph as it rolls along the bottom. The only slack you want is what the ''90-degree'' angle coming off the rod tip produces.

Finally, **adjust your leader and weights and nymphs to get your point nymph down on the bottom where the fish are.**

You can't always follow each and every one of these rules. Out on the stream one rule sometimes conflicts with another. Sometimes you have to compromise, lose touch with your nymph a little maybe, to get the bottom-roll you want, or get closer to the fish than you'd like to, to avoid some dragging currents between you and the water you want to cover . . . in general, however, the above rules are the key ones for nymphing, and the better you can follow them the better your chances of success.

I've shot a shallow tuck upstream, and now I'm picking up the slack that's in my line and I'm getting ready to lift my rod tip as the drift starts back to me over the bottom. When you make a cast of some distance you don't want to pick up too fast. Give that weighted nymph a moment to settle to the bottom before you lift. It's a continuous motion: check-the-cast-and-your-nymph-enters-the-water-and-you-start-to-pick-up . . . but it's gradual, giving that nymph time to settle. If I lift too fast I'll lift the nymph out of the business district—there might be a good fish there, at the entry of the cast. I want to be in touch with that nymph the whole way through the cast and the drift, but I want to give it a chance to settle to the bottom too, before I lift.

45

I've picked up the slack and started to lift the rod tip. My line's coming down from my rod tip at that ''90-degree'' angle—roughly 90 degrees to the rod— roughly 90 degrees to the water—that I want to maintain. If the line starts to drift back in under my rod I've got too much slack—I won't feel the fish and if I do I'll have too much line on the water to make a hook-up when I strike. It's a delicate balance and I concentrate on maintaining it . . .

. . . as my nymph drifts and bounces back downstream over the bottom toward me. I'm stripping line, preserving that "90-degree" angle from rod to line, lifting, stripping, lifting, stripping as the drift comes back to me—*I'm leading my nymph with my rod tip the whole way through the drift.* I'm concentrating on my line on the water and where the end of my leader enters the water and the feel of the line in my hands and rod. If I see or feel the slightest hesitation, the slightest touch or pause in the bottom-roll—if I see the slightest hesitation of my line on the water . . .

. . . I strike. My rod lifts as I set the hook. When you've kept in touch with your fly throughout the drift you don't need to over-lift to set the hook.

Get an angle on that fish right away. I've angled my rod to the left to exert side-pressure to keep the fish off balance.

I reach down and gently take the fly between my thumb and forefinger and twist it and release the trout in the water. I'm using a barbless hook, which I highly recommend.

Be flexible. If you must fish across-stream, do it. But *lift your line over as many current changes as possible.* I'm fishing out and across-stream. The depth, speed, and clarity of the water dictate my approach. The currents here are deep—they're fast, and the water isn't exceptionally clear so I can risk getting a little closer to the water I want to fish. Now I don't have as many current changes between me and the fish. With my longer rod I'm able to lift my line up over the current changes between me and the water I'm fishing. The more currents you can work around—position yourself to avoid and lift your rod over, the longer, better, more natural drift you'll get.

Don't let the fish see you. Keep your profile low—kneel down in the water if you have to. The water here is slower, shallower, and a little bit more clear, so I'm staying just as low as I possibly can as I shoot a modified tuck in tight to the brush along the bank. I've made the check and my nymph is dropping in at an angle.

As the drift commences I'm in tight touch with my line and fly—rod and line make the "90-degree" angle. *Lift your line over as many currents as possible: with a long rod I'm able to lift off the varying currents in front of me as I fish the velocity change,* the spot where slower and faster water meet. In this case the velocity change is in tight to the brush along the bank where the streambottom deepens—you can see it from the darker color of the water I've cast to.

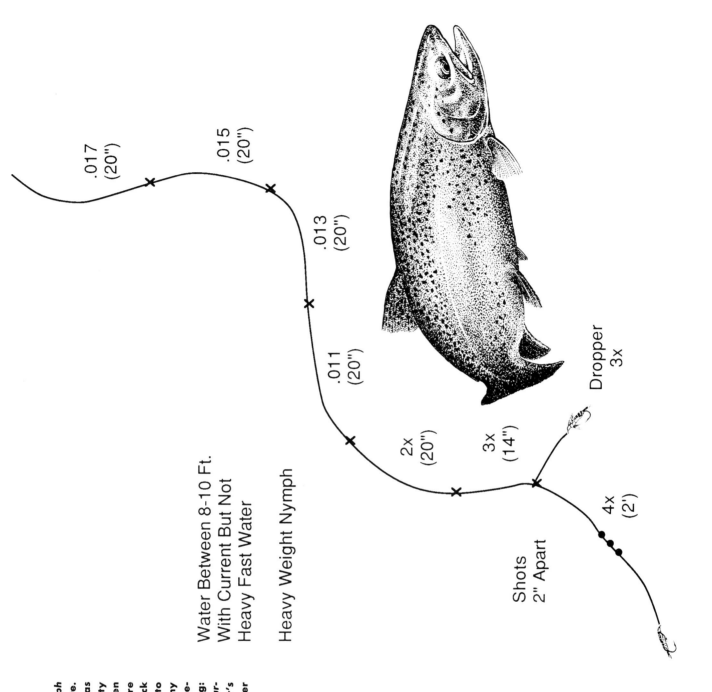

.017
(20")

.015
(20")

.013
(20")

.011
(20")

2x
(20")

3x
(14")

Dropper
3x

4x
(2')

Shots
2" Apart

Water Between 8-10 Ft.
With Current But Not
Heavy Fast Water

Heavy Weight Nymph

Adjust your rig to get your point nymph down on the bottom. Faster water here. Deeper water. So I might be rigged as shown below. I'm casting to the velocity change where the flatter, less broken surface-flow meets slightly more broken water. I've made a rolling tuck and lifted my hands high at the finish to drive the nymph down in. I've lifted my line up over the current changes between me and the water I'm fishing: Keep your line away from as many current changes as possible. This water's discolored, so I figured I could get closer without the fish seeing me. . . .

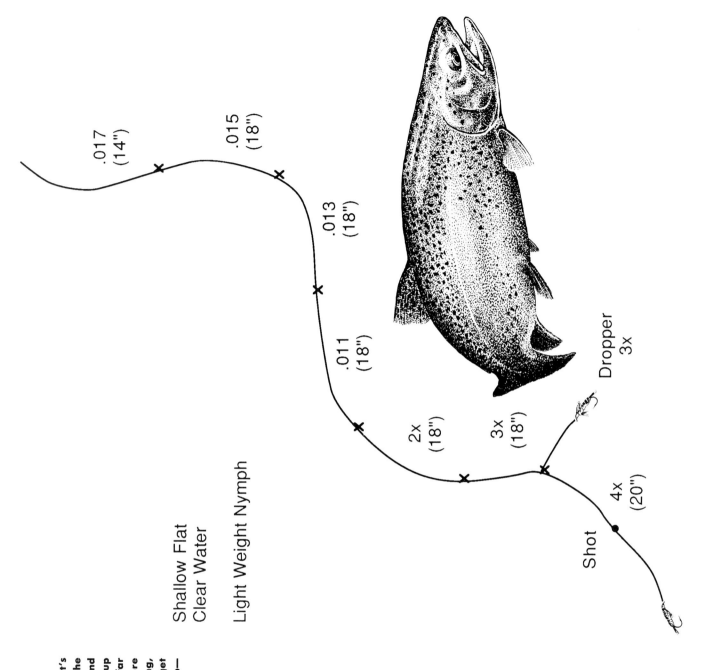

.017
(14")

.015
(18")

.013
(18")

.011
(18")

Shallow Flat
Clear Water

Light Weight Nymph

2x
(18")

3x
(18")

Dropper
3x

Shot

4x
(20")

Adjust! Here the current's slower. It's shallower, clearer—I've changed to the rig shown below. I'm crouched low and I'm shooting a very shallow tuck way up to the head of the pool. Look how far forward I've drifted my rod before squeezing off the check to get that long, shallow tuck. I'm ready to pick up—get the excess slack in and lift the rod tip—after my nymph enters the water.

Here's another situation, a nice pocket, right in front of me—the water's a little off-color so I've moved in from the side, a bit closer, but not too close. I've sent my nymph to the head of the pocket and my nymph tucks in where the broken water meets the smoother water-surface: velocity change. My rod tip has started to lift and I've smoothly stripped all excess slack out of my line. My line's up off the current changes in between me and the drift to avoid drag. I'm starting to lead the drift, the bottom-roll, of my nymph with my rod tip. I'm in a crouch. All my attention is on that line and leader and the feel of my nymph as it's starting to roll and bounce downstream over the bottom. I'm going to fish my nymph down along the side of the pocket, down along the velocity change where broken water meets smoother water . . .

58

. . . what keeps me in touch, what gives me that excellent hooking power when a fish inhales, is that I'm stripping line in—leading that drift with my rod—keeping in close contact with my nymph throughout the drift . . . you can see the velocity change, where one current-speed meets a different current-speed, right at the bottom of the photo. If I see or feel a bump, a hesitation, pressure, anything at all that seems to interrupt the natural drift of my nymph, I strike. I'm ready to slip-strike here, a combination of stripping line *and* lifting the rod. I'm using a combination of stripping and a hand-twist retrieve, fine-tuning the retrieve to accommodate the slightest slowing of the current in front of me. . . .

I've put the hook to the fish and the fish races to the tail of the pool. Look at my casting hand pointing upstream—I've immediately pointed my rod away from the fish, angled my rod across my body to get side-pressure, to get an angle on the trout. I trap my line against my rod with my casting hand and my non-casting hand is starting to reel the slack line back on my reel. You can see the velocity change quite clearly, the imprecise border where faster water meets slower water, running down through the pocket to where the fish is fighting.

Top photo: He makes a little run. *Bottom photo:* Lifting my rod tip to get an angle on its head to keep it off-balance, I lift the fish back, stripping in line.

I get that side-pressure on him again right away *(above),* with my rod pointing upstream and away from the fish . . . I'm stripping in line, keeping the pressure smoothly, firmly on him, keeping him off balance . . . I keep that side-pressure, that angle, on him right up to landing him *(top-left photo, facing page)* . . . a nice little brookie. If I've positioned myself to get a good angle on the fish from the beginning, if I've eliminated excess slack, if I've kept myself in good close contact with my nymph throughout the drift, I've set myself up to hook and play the fish successfully.

Fish the velocity change. This is heavy water, swift and deep. You can see many velocity changes, corridors of flow—strips of broken current and strips of smoother current between them. The cast has sent the nymph to a strip of slower water that will give my nymph time to settle to the bottom without my having to add weight. A long rod and a good tuck will get my line and leader out over the currents in between me and the fish. I've sent my cast to water that will give my medium-weighted nymph time to get to the bottom: the darker, smoother strip of water just out from the broken water flowing, in turn, just out from the smooth current running in along the far bank. . . .

I keep control of the line, stripping, elevating my rod tip, leading the nymph through the drift, keeping my line over as many currents as possible, giving my nymph a good roll—a *long* roll—over the bottom. Sinking lines are difficult to handle in this type of water. They belly and drag and it's impossible to get good control from rod tip to nymph.

Often anglers will skip water like this, or wade through it to get to the pool. But there could be good fish here. In pockets, behind boulders where the velocity changes exist, at the edge of currents, and in the dark patches of water that signify a velocity change, one technique that has been very effective for me over the years is to work these small pockets and velocity changes with short casts, a downer-upper, or a short tuck that sends the nymph in at a sharp angle. The rod tip remains elevated as the nymph drives in.

The drift is brief. Don't wait for the obvious take. Blind-strike. In a short small pocket you don't have time to wait. It's unbelievable how fast a trout can mouth a nymph and eject it. In a short drift, even with line control, you often can't detect the take. If you blind-strike in conditions like this, you will surprise yourself at how often you're into a fish.

You must constantly *adjust your weights and weighted nymphs and tippet to get your nymph down on the bottom* and tailor your presentation and drift to get that natural roll over the bottom. At times you will hang up. If you're not hanging up part of the time you're not nymphing properly. So it behooves you to learn to free your nymph when this happens, and I've got a couple ways of doing this. For starters you can roll cast . . .

. . . upstream beyond the hang up; your line passes the nymph or hang up—i.e. goes upstream of where you're stuck on the bottom . . .

Lift sharply. Often your hook will come free. (Try this trick sharply and *fast*—do it the *instant* you realize you've hung up.)

Or you can wade up to where you're stuck and reach down in the water with your rod—point the rod straight down into the stream all the way to your nymph. Slip the eye of your rod tip up against the fly or the hook bend of your fly and most of the time you'll be able to nudge it free of the obstruction . . . same principle works if you're hung up in a tree . . .

. . . if all else fails either you have to break off or you gotta get wet. But whatever you do don't worry about hanging up on the bottom. If you're fishing the nymph properly it's going to happen. You've got to take chances, get down on the bottom with the nymph, try to cast in under that tree or into that brush pile. If you start backing off from tough stream situations you will never develop the confidence to tackle difficult areas that can result in more fish landed. You'll probably be saving flies but you'll be missing fish. Another thing to remember, when you're hung up and you get free, *check that fly*—if it's picked up the least bit of vegetation or debris of any kind, they won't touch it.

I'm concentrating on what's happening, on what is before me, the picture unfolds—I'm fishing at an angle, off to the side, I'm in control of my line from rod tip to nymph, my rod tip's up, I've lowered my profile, I've got my line up over the current changes. I'm working the velocity change at the lower left of the photo. Trout will lie in faster water if they have obstructions on the bottom they can get behind. Make the approach. Make the weight adjustment. Check your nymph. Lower your profile. Make your cast . . . lift, accelerate, *tap*, drift forward—*tap*. Lift your rod, strip the slack in, *concentrate*—lead the drift with your rod tip, be alert for the slightest hesitation or pause . . . I may sound like a broken record as I go through all this but these points are vitally important to success. You've got to work at it. You've got to keep punching away at it. That tough little pocket you're thinking of skipping and saying "Ah, the heck with it" might just hold the best fish of the day. . . .

69

Leading the nymph with the rod tip keeps the belly out of your line, keeps you in touch with what's happening on the bottom. You're not pulling the nymph. You're guiding it. In leading it with the rod tip you're keeping it moving over the bottom at a natural speed, meaning you're not going to let it hang. If the water's slow and your nymph isn't making normal progress you can lead it—with the rod tip—faster than the currents are flowing and still maintain a natural drift. Sometimes with a weighted nymph getting that natural speed takes a little extra persuasion with the rod tip. You lift just enough to keep that nymph rolling naturally over the bottom. Dry flies on the surface must float at the speed of the current. But many nymphs wriggle, they swim, they pulsate and squirm and bounce—they speed up and slow down, they sink and rise. So if your nymph does happen to make a jump or move different from the speed and direction of the current, it's all right. It can be a technique. When you're nymphing upstream try letting 'em rise and fall, let them drop on the downstream drift and lift them for the rise. That little bit of movement might turn the day for you. Do it with two nymphs—the dropper looks like an emerger trying to get to the surface—your point nymph looks like a nymph trying to get off the bottom. You want total control of that line and those nymphs at all times.

Leading—guiding—your nymph with your rod tip, keeping in tight touch with your fly, watching your leader for the slightest hesitation—*feeling* for the slightest pause or hesitation that might be a fish mouthing your nymph, watching for the flash of a trout turning, you're poised to strike. A lot of people talk about strike indicators. I don't use them. I don't recommend them. The main reason I don't care for the strike indicator is that you tend to become mesmerized by it—you're watching the indicator on your line to the neglect of all the other factors you need to be thinking of: line control, leading with your tip, stripping line, feeling, using that sixth sense. Staring at a strike indicator as your drift comes back to you you can miss a heck of a lot else that's going on. Once in a while with a beginner who has no idea what to look for and no concept of what's going on, a strike indicator may be all right. Or when shooting or covering distance a strike indicator may be the only way visually to be in touch with the nymph. On an extended downstream drift an indicator can help you keep a nymph drifting at a specific level and enhance visibility. But the indicator can become a crutch and worse, tune you out to all the other things you need to be paying attention to.

. . . if I let my nymph get this far past me I'm probably not doing much good. My nymph's too close to me. However, if you don't have a lot of water clarity, you can fish out the cast. A fish may take as your nymph lifts off the bottom downstream of you.

The moral of the story is, *Lead your nymph with your rod tip the whole way through the drift.* Above I'm leading my nymph more or less from the side—keeping my rod tip ahead—in other words downstream—of my nymph as I fish the drift out.

When I'm nymphing directly upstream, leading the nymph with the rod tip means lifting . . .

. . . lifting my rod tip ahead . . .

. . . of my nymph as it comes rolling over the bottom downstream to me. If you keep in close touch and guide the nymph over the bottom while keeping at all times attuned to the drift . . .

. . . you'll be prepared to set that hook with maximum effectiveness. Here's striking-and-playing again . . . my eyes are on that fish. I've immediately gotten my rod at an angle to the fish and I'm keeping the trout off balance and with my line trapped against my rod with my casting hand I can reel in slack with my other hand . . .

. . . side pressure—line trapped against rod with casting hand (I'm a lefty remember) . . . look how my non-casting hand has slid a foot or so up that rod and is holding it, shortening it in effect, making it a 7-footer instead of an 8-footer, enabling me to put more pressure on, get more leverage on the fish.

A LOT OF THESE BASIC PRINCIPLES APPLY TO MORE THAN ONE TECH-
nique or situation. As I've pointed out, *leading your nymph through the drift with
your rod tip* can mean one thing when you're nymphing upstream and another
when you're fishing across-stream. When your nymph is coming directly downstream back to you, leading with the tip means lifting that tip up. When you're
fishing across, leading with the tip means moving the tip to the side and lifting
downstream—keeping it ahead of the nymph.

Fish the velocity changes means cast to those places where there is a change
in the current speed—this can mean a change in depth, a change in what's on
the bottom—a big underwater rock or other obstruction such as vegetation—or
a change in current direction, like a backeddy.

Don't let the fish see you can mean keeping the sun behind you. It can mean
concealing yourself under overhanging branches. It can mean crouching, keeping your profile low, kneeling right down in the current if you have to.

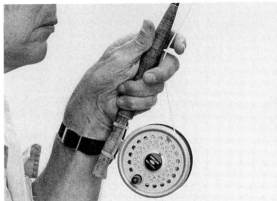

Lift your line over as many current changes as possible might mean going to
a longer rod, nine feet, even ten. It might mean using that rod to lift out over the
drag-producing currents between you and the fish. It might mean positioning,
getting yourself at an angle that avoids the maximum number of current
changes.

These fundamentals sometimes come into conflict with each other. You might
have to risk a fish seeing you or you might have to shoot at a greater distance
than you ordinarily would in order to get the angle you want. You might have to
give up the ideal angle because the water's too clear. When the water's too
deep or fast your ability to position may be restricted. You're changing all the
time, changing approach, angle, cast, retrieve. It's a drama. Some parts are
light, some heavy—you have your ups and downs, your highs and lows, all
kinds of changes, and you relate to them, damn near emotionally. You get a feel
for each area, each pool, each run, each pocket. You're staying with it, you're
going to the trouble to make the weight adjustment, or to go to a heavier or a
lighter nymph, or to rebuild your tippet, or the whole leader if that's what's
called for.

You keep working at it, you keep moving, changing . . . if you've achieved a
good bottom drift through a given pocket or pool and nothing happens, don't
camp on it—move on. Try the next patch of water. If they don't take your nymph
on the first couple passes your odds are dramatically lowered. Don't stand in
one place mindlessly making the same great cast and drift again and again. The
more water you cover and the more fish you fish over, the better your chances of
taking fish.

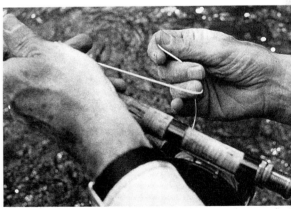

You make the approach and you get into position and you make the correct
cast—if your rig's wrong, fix it. Do what you have to to get your nymph down
there rolling over the bottom in just as natural a fashion as you can manage.
Keep in close touch with it—rod tip leading your nymph, eyes on your line, hands
and fingers controlling your slack and feeling for that pause, that slightest hesitation. It's part instinct, a sixth sense—if your drift suddenly feels odd, strike.

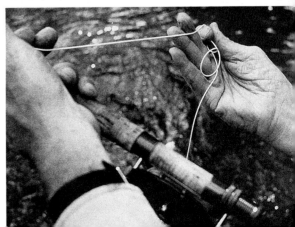

Tricos in
the Rain

ONE BIG THING ABOUT NYMPHING IS KNOWING WHEN TO DO IT. IF they're rising but your dry fly isn't producing, or if you're floating a dry fly over them but they're not coming up, *change*. Rig with a nymph and go under the water—keep experimenting!

On the following pages we have a graphic demonstration of how experimentation can pay off. Conditions are tough. The trout are surface-feeding only sporadically. It's raining a little, and, unfortunately . . .

. . . it's foggy.

I'm starting out with a dry fly. The summer-morning Trico hatch is beginning to come off and I'm fishing a #20 dry in that pattern. I'm rolling it out into the main current where they're intermittently feeding. I'm casting from the bank. You can see (above) I've lifted my rod tip up and back behind me to swing that line, bellying, behind me so the belly can load the rod as I get ready to . . .

. . . squeeze that powerstroke with a short check *(above)*. It's quite a fast, short, powerful move—my rod's bent double—you can see the roll starting *(below)*. My rod having unloaded, the energy is traveling right out through my line . . .

. . . with my loop climbing—unfolding at an angle up away from the water—so it'll stop and drop at the end of the cast delivering my leader to the water with the S-curves I want in it (more on this when we get to dry flies).

THEY'VE REFUSED MY #20 TRICO. MAYBE IT'S THE FOG. LIGHT RAIN won't put fish down but if you get a low fog on the water you can be in trouble. The hatch doesn't really seem to be on either. I'm going to try something else.

I'm going to tie on a #10 deer-hair ant and work it in tight to the banks, in around the branches and the trees and brush. The reason I'm going to try the ant is that later in the morning, when the Trico hatch is over, they feed on terrestrials. It's conditioning. As the earth starts to warm up around mid-morning terrestrials start to move. Throughout mountain country such as we're in here, carpenter ants are part of the trout's diet. So, even though it's not midday yet, I know those trout are *conditioned* to the ant, and I'm thinking let's see if that ant will trigger a response. I'm cutting my tippet back as I go to the heavier fly. I'm going to wade upstream to a different spot. If they start to pop on those Tricos while I'm fishing my terrestrial I'll change back. I'm constantly experimenting, changing. . . .

The lower of the two ants in the photo below has been fished many a time and it's banged up and torn apart but that's all right. They'll take it anyway. It has shape, liveliness.

I've waded upstream and I'm going to cast my ant in tight to that bank, in to the left of those branches, a good, sheltered spot for a fish. A good place for ants and other terrestrials to be falling onto the water. I'm getting ready to make a roll cast into the bank to the left of those branches. Lifting my rod tip I've swung the belly of line behind me . . . I'm ready for the forward drift and powerstroke. This cast will have a modification in it, an adjustment to the stream situation I'm facing.

Here's the powerstroke. I've fired a short, compact stroke. See how my elbow's starting to tuck in? My line's starting to roll out on the forecast toward the target. I've pushed my thumb up into the cast to open the loop wider, to put slack into the leader. As my line continues to unroll I'm going to cut a bit of a hook and mend off the roll to send my fly out to the left, to the left of those branches. I'm going to change the direction of the rod tip, bringing my casting hand across to the right . . .

... to throw my line out to the left. Compare where my hand is in this photo to the previous photo. I've hooked my wrist to the right and this move pulls the portion of line traveling out from my rod tip—pulls that moving line to the right, which causes a reaction, out at the business end of that moving line. The business end of the line is thrown *left*—you can see it. For every action there's an equal and opposite reaction. This is a law of physics and it's a law of fly-casting too. Action, reaction. Loaded rod bends *backward* and when you check it unloads *forward*. Action, reaction. When you lift the rod *up* at the end of a Rolling Tuck you're driving that nymph *down*. And here *(above photo)*, as I throw the hook and mend I want my line to go out to the *left* so I move that rod tip to the *right*. Once the energy's generated and going out through the line you can move the rod to give that line . . .

... direction. Rod tip moves right—upstream—to send line and fly downstream to the left of, and in beyond, those branches. Try it with a piece of string. Hold a three-foot piece of string, letting it dangle until it hangs still. Stand up to do this so you can look down at it. Now abruptly cut your wrist left or right. Watch how the impulse travels the string. Now try it with the string moving. Hold the string high and let it dangle until it's still. Now drop it, drop it down—fast—and as you do so cut your wrist sharply left or right. Watch what the end of the string does. Action, reaction. In the photo above the impulse of the hook and mend has pretty much left the portion of line coming out from my rod tip and is out at the far end of the line.

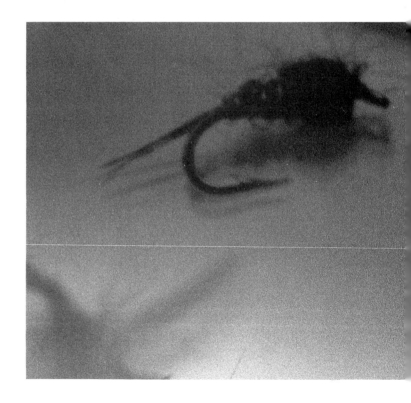

See where the cast delivered my line (above)? Notice I've lowered my rod—made a level-change. But no fish. They aren't interested in my deer-hair ant. One reason they're not coming up might be because they're not *looking* up. There is not enough terrestrial activity to move them to the top. I'm not going to camp on it—time to try something else. That hatch hasn't really gotten underway . . . but an occasional Trico dun tells me there is nymphal activity underneath—the fish have been conditioned to nymphal activity from this hatch for the last few weeks. So I take that dry fly off and change to a nymph. I'm going to try a tiny one, a Number 22 Trico . . . I'm going to get back downstream on the bank and rollcast to the center current where they're hanging. I'm going to fish it just under the surface. With such a small nymph I'll stay with my dry-fly leader-and-tippet combo. I want to keep thinking and analyzing, experimenting with different approaches, figuring those fish out. . . .

Here's the roll. Look at that line sliding back over the water toward me and lifting up into the belly hanging down from my rod as I lift my rod out behind me, lift that rod tip and lift as much line as possible off the water, then drift the casting hand to about the level of my ear, preparatory to the powerstroke.

Here's the powerstroke forward *(above)* and the beginning of the roll out over the water *(below)*. Action, reaction. Water's low and clear even though it's raining, sprinkling a little, so it behooves me to stay on the bank, as far away from those fish as possible . . . look at that loop!

My elbow came in—my hand has done its job and stopped—the rod has done its job and stopped . . . now the line's doing the job. I have control of the line. I've dropped my rod-level to help collapse the leader . . .

. . . so I'll get a drag-free float out there . . . the cast is finished and I'm starting to strip a bit, I'm controlling the line and keeping any excess slack out of it. Notice the "90-degree" angle.

I'VE HAD TO SHOOT LINE FOR DISTANCE *(FACING PAGE)*, TO STAY OUT of sight of the fish. I've lowered my elbow and rod tip at the end of the roll to collapse my leader and get those nice coils—S-curves—in my leader up to the fly to give me that natural, drag-free drift.

A couple other thoughts. First, that wasn't a perfect roll cast I just made. My loop wasn't picture perfect, but the cast did exactly what I wanted it to. It shot forty-five or fifty feet of line out to that main current where they're hanging, and it brought that leader down collapsed, instead of straightened out and dragging. Also, notice how I kept my hand on my line the whole way through the cast—I was casting to a very limited and specific area, a run of current where the trout are holding.

They're starting to move out there . . . I've moved a couple fish on that nymph. It's drifting just under the surface naturally . . . but something's not quite right. It's not exactly what they want . . . I've got to try and figure them out. . . .

The fog has drifted off the water. This is good news. I've never done well with fog on the water.

They're spooky. The Trico hatch isn't really going full force and they're being very, very particular. They can be had, but they're tough.

If they're feeding at all, a nymph is a good bet.

The saying attributed to the American Indian, and related to me by Don Keppler, goes something like: ''Turkey see, turkey go. Turkey hear, turkey go. Turkey no see and no hear, turkey go anyway.''

I say, If you see nothing on top, go under. If you see a few rises, go under anyway. And if you see a lot of rises, *still* go under with a nymph—the biggest fish is down there.

It's difficult . . . I've got to pay attention to what I'm doing and keep trying different combos, different flies, different drifts and floats, to see if I can figure 'em out.

Now they're starting to pop. They're starting to rise out there. I saw three fish break. They're starting to move. Maybe that hatch is finally getting serious.

I've got to be flexible—here comes the change. I'm going back to my #20 Trico on the surface. Let's see if it produces . . . okay trout, say your prayers. . . .

YOU NOTICE MY LINE'S RELATIVELY STRAIGHT. YOU HEAR ABOUT THE Snake Cast or the Lazy-S Cast, which puts curves in your line to absorb the current changes, but what good are curves in your line if your leader's straightened out? We'll get into this in detail later but I mention it now because it's so important: Cast that dry fly so your leader and tippet collapse and lay down on the water in S-curves right out to your fly. It's the only way to get a natural, drag-free float. I'm not saying *don't* cast curves in your line, but you've got to get coils and curves in your leader and tippet in addition or the fly's going to start dragging the moment it comes down. There are a lot of subtle little current changes out there in the middle where my fly's riding. S-curves in my leader and tippet, right out to the fly, are a must.

Let's review the situation. We've seen fish break, although very sporadically, so we know there's interest in the trout population. This spring-fed water's on the cool side, 56°, so they're feeding less than they might normally. The fog didn't help either. And something else—a front came in last evening and that barometer's down. Even though they're conditioned to feed, they can feel that pressure-change. The drop in pressure can slow them down.

Surface feeding very sporadic. So the majority of the trout population is still down on the bottom. Water's temperature's low. Hatching activity's limited, but it's there. Conditioning. Always think conditioning—what are those trout used to? They've been conditioned to that Trico hatch every morning for many weeks (this is late summer)—it's like a conditioned reflex.

The fish are moving, the hatch is coming off, though not dramatically. Those fish are taking something . . . I'll tell you one thing they're not taking, they're not taking my #20 Trico on the surface. They're moving though—I moved a couple on that little nymph when I was drifting it just under the surface. Now. I've noticed that when I give my dry fly a bit of motion, twitch it a little, they move for it. It's that conditioned response—when I move that sucker they've got a notion to take. But they don't take it. It's more like a refusal at the last minute than any kind of take. To twitch the fly I've pulled the slack out of the leader up to the fly and gotten immediate drag—one reason for the refusal. But it's evidence. It's a piece of information, a piece of the puzzle I'm piecing together. It tells me they're feeding on movement. They're feeding on movement but not on the surface. So I'm going back under.

I'm going to try a larger nymph, a number 18 Trico nymph, and I'm going to fish it with a little movement. It's a bit larger than the size of nymph they're probably feeding on but it has shape, color, silhouette, movement, and most important *I can get it down to the fish.*

It's going to resemble a Trico nymph coming up to the surface, at least I hope it is. I've rebuilt my leader and I'm putting on a very little bit of split-shot and I'm going to fish my nymph moving it very slightly, trying different ways of giving it motion.

You've got to keep changing and experimenting, observing, putting the pieces of the puzzle together. . . .

I think they're slashing on the rise, taking that nymph when it's on the move—up.

I give it a long, soft presentation.

With that very small piece of shot positioned about twelve inches up from my nymph I'm getting a good sink rate.

I give it time to sink—I think it's getting down there near the bottom, but not *quite* to the bottom. . . .

I watch the leader as it's sinking, and when it's almost to the bottom I strip just a little and lift, slowly . . .

. . . my nymph lifts in the water . . .

. . . bingo. I've figured 'em out. It's a bit of a slip-strike. I'm stripping line to set the hook. They weren't coming up for that #22 when I was drifting it just under the surface. Had I gone with a weighted nymph earlier I'd've been into fish a lot sooner, but I had to figure it out step by step.

Hopefully I have 'em figured for now. Maybe I can start catching fish.

Wasn't that something? I just—I love this. That's why I want to fish every day and learn. A year to go . . .

. . . before I retire. Then I'll really have the time to go out and learn something about this game. Trap that line against that rod with your casting hand and reel in that slack as you . . .

. . . keep a good angle on the fish—shorten the rod—get leverage . . . keep that fish off balance . . .

. . . you're patiently, relaxedly having a good time playing the fish. At the same time you want to get that fish in as quickly . . .

. . . as possible so the fish isn't exhausted when you release him.

You're concentrating but you're not tensed—poised—the way you are when you're fishing out a float or drift and waiting for that hit.

I'll fish every day and really try to learn this game . . .

. . . reach in with the thumb . . .

. . . and forefinger . . .

. . . whoops. You net the fish or beach it if you want to keep it—I hardly ever keep a trout anymore.

Take hold of that fly, I was going to say—but I've decided to pick him up by his . . .

. . . jaw. My Number 18 Trico nymph is right where I'm pointing, caught right through the side of his mouth where I stuck it to him when he inhaled. A nice native brown. I had to work for him.

Nymphing Tips

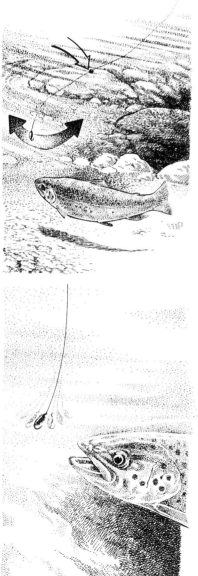

AN OLD TRICK I'VE USED FOR YEARS WHEN SIGHT FISHING IS TO LET the nymph just lie there. You lay your cast out so your weight, which you've got 6 or 8 inches up from your nymph, hangs on a rock or on some elodea and you let it hang there and let the currents swing that nymph back and forth. It drives 'em crazy. You're waiting, back out of sight. Be patient. He's looking at that nymph. The currents are moving that fly back and forth, back and forth in place—you might have to wait two, three minutes. He's gonna look at that nymph and finally he can't stand it and here he comes—he drives right in and takes. There are just a million ways to fish. Be your own person. Experiment . . . there are times when you don't even need to cast, you can work the nymph on the bottom with limited line and leader.

Try a terrestrial, a cricket or an ant, a deer-hair ant with a little weight tied in—fish it in that summertime pocket just the way you would a nymph. Terrestrials fall in and they drift to the fish just as a nymph would.

Watch where that line picks up, watch where it goes tight when you lift that tip. If it picks up high in the pocket that shows you your nymphs are getting down there where they're supposed to be and they're getting there on time. If you're not on the bottom immediately, put more weight on, or send your nymph in at a steeper angle, or adjust the weights, or a combination of these.

At the same time you don't want to lift too fast, especially on a long shallow tuck. Give the nymph a little time to settle down to the bottom, then lift. You have to do it a thousand times, then you start to get the feel . . . check your fly, make sure there's nothing on it. If you see any hesitation, if that drift looks or feels the least bit funny, don't wait—strike!

Remember, good trout can lie in inches of water. Cover those shallow stretches, shoot a little more line, take your weight off. Going into deeper water, deeper pockets, tie on something bigger, heavier. Conditions may dictate you make the weight change with the nymph rather than on the leader. Lift over the current changes. Position yourself to cast around those current changes.

Make the weight adjustment, but before you do, look to see if there's water nearby you might want to cover with the set-up you already have, before you change. I'm looking at a deep run and I know I'm going to have to add weight to get down for this depth, but before I do maybe I better step off to the side, to the shallower portion of the pocket, and cover it—*then* change to go deeper.

▲
The rod is loaded for a rolling tuck cast.

▶
The cast is short with the rod tip lifting as the nymph drops in.

▶
The rod tip remains elevated and line control is established immediately. The drift was short and this trout took in the velocity change directly in front of me.

▲
A foot long native brown.

▲
With a barbless hook, the fish is easily released by a twist of the thumb and forefinger.

▼
When working the dry fly you want to lift around as many currents as possible for a good drag-free float.

▲
A low profile is imperative in shallow, clear water. Stay back as far as you can from the fish, yet close enough to lift over the major currents for an extended drag-free float—particularly if this is your only option for position.

◄
This hefty rainbow fell to a Cressbug imitation—Cressbugs and scuds are prolific in this limestone spring-fed tributary. Notice the bright green duck weed in the background and the green watercress around me, indicators of cold spring water.

▶

Trout hang close to cover. Nymphing techniques, if the water isn't too clear, might mean working two foot of leader off the end of the rod. Work the nymph under and around the debris.

▶

A short casting stroke, rod tip up, and line control in tight to the log.

▶

And one was there!

▲
With side pressure on the trout, I keep the fish off balance and lead it away from the cover.

▶
Now I have the freedom to land the fish.

◀ A chunky native brown trout.

▲ Tandem Bucktail Streamer. Use for big fish day or night.

▲ Both duck weed *(top right)* and watercress *(lower left)* indicate cold water and can be used to locate spring holes.

▶ George Harvey Night Fly (Pusher Fly). Use with #4, #2, #1, #1/0, #2/0 hooks. Body is fur and palmered. Wings are doubled on each side: goose breast and pheasant breast feathers. Fish down and across with a very slow retrieve: Count to three, then lift the rod top and repeat the process throughout the drift.

▼ Wooley Worm *(top)*. Use #10 hook. This caddis worm imitation can imitate the dragonfly nymph or any nymphal movement.

The other flies are Wooley Buggers, tied with both chenille and fur bodies and heavily palmered: marabou tails, heavy head hackles. These provide lots of movement and can imitate a variety of nymphal or sculpin activity. Fish by using nymphing or sculpin techniques day or night. The Wooley Buggers rolled on the bottom after dark are good for big fish.

▼ Sulphur Nymph Imitations, used with #12, #14, #16 hooks are weighted and flattened causing a rocking motion when the currents wash over the flattened

surface of the nymph. They are fished at two levels: point nymph on the bottom and with a dropper for an emerger. *(Top)* Used with a #16 hook: tail of partridge; body is light brown fur, ribbed with brass wire and flattened; thorax of dark fur; wings (on both sides) of partridge. *(Center)* Same tie used with #12 hook. *(Bottom)* Same tie except emu fibers are tied in the body. Protruding from the top to imitate gills, they add movement to the nymph. No. 12 hook.

▼

Stonefly series. *(Top row, right)* For #4, #2, #1 hooks, 3X long shank. Wing of calf tail; body is yellow chenille, palmered with brown hackle; brown head hackle. *(Top row, center)* Heavily palmered with dark brown body, heavy head hackle, and no wing. *(Top row, left)* Tied the same as top right except for orange body and yellow calf tail wing.

These three flies are fished when stonefly hatches are on. Work in close to banks and around mid-stream boulders, using the down and across techniques that impart movement to rod tip. Use during nighttime hatching activity. Wet fly techniques can be deadly.

The three flies on the right, bottom row, are different sizes of the Harvey Stonefly. The second from the right has a palmered body. Use with #10, #8, #6 hooks. See page 69 of *Joe Humphreys's Trout Tactics* for how to tie. The last two flies *(lower left)* are Wooley Bugger ties.

For fishing the flies in the bottom row, use the nymphing technique. The tuck cast and upstream technique can also be used. With weight attached above two trailing flies or nymphs, roll on the bottom with out and across downstream roll.

▲

Green Drake and Hexigenia, large wet flies (used with #6 or #4 hooks), imitate the larger mayfly hatches and are most effective after dark when these hatches are in progress. Use the down and across technique with a pulsating-rod-tip movement. Also used upstream with a natural drift. The Green Drake and/or Hexigenia Wet Fly *(top right)* is made of soft, absorbent materials that impart lots of movement in the water: wings of calf tail; body of fur with a palmer; hackle, hen; ribbing, brass wire. *(Lower left)* Wings of duck quill; body of fur with palmer; hackle, hen; ribbing, brass wire. When fishing either the Stonefly series or the Green Drake series, start with the nymphs, and then in the last stage of the hatching activity work the wet flies, at night.

▲

Feather and marabou streamers *(top row)*. Use with #1 or #1/0 hooks. These can work the water for big fish with varied streamer tactics: lifting, jerking retrieve at different speeds of natural bottom drift, or roll the bottom with an occasional lift throughout the drift.

Ed Shenk Sculpins *(bottom row)*. Snub lead shot on nose of sculpin. Bounce and lift off the bottom. Retrieve at different speeds depending on the water temperature: Slow down in cold water; with summer temperatures or temps in the 60s, move the fly faster.

▲

Green Drake Wet Flies and Nymphs. *(Top left)* Wet fly for #4 hook: body of yellow chenille palmered with light brown hackle, wing of calf tail, brown hackle. Fish this one after dark across and down stream. Bounce the rod tip and impart movement throughout the swing.

(Top right) Same as previous except body is fur. For #6 and #8, 2X or 3X long shank hooks. Fish the same as previous. This one can also be fished through the day with the same night techniques or straight upstream as you would a nymph except that you straighten the cast.

(Center, left and right) Humphreys Green Drake Nymph. Tail of soft fibers from hen hackle (color straw); body, a blend of light yellow with light brown fur; emu feathers for gills; wing case of turkey wing fibers; light brown head hackle. For the tying technique, see page 70 of my book *Joe Humphreys's Trout Tactics*. Can be fished day and night. Roll the bottom. Use tuck cast and nymphing techniques.

(Bottom) For #8 or #6 hooks, 3X long shank. Tying technique is the same except body fur is spun loosely so the body is bulkier and more absorbent, giving more movement. For night nymphing, this one is fished on the bottom and/or lifted off the bottom with a pulsating tip action.

▲

Some of my favorites. *Top left:* Humphreys Green Drake Nymph. In the early 1950s I decided to find out what the green drake nymphs really looked like. I found them in the gravel and sediment of the riffles, took a few home, and went to work at the tying bench. A couple of weeks before the proposed hatching time, I examined the bottom of the stream, and at first sighting of the adult nymph, I nymphed the bottom with outstanding success.

The nymph varies in color from straw to pale yellow. I blend light brown and yellow rabbit fur for the abdomen and the head, emu fibers for the gills, mottled turkey wing folded for the wing case, and a pair of ginger hackles intermixed for the legs.

Top center: Humphreys Caddis Pupa. A good first-hand look at a caddis pupa prompted this tie. To give the pupa imitation a natural look with lots of movement, tie peacock herl in at either end of the pupa and a heavy palmer of dark brown hackle over the fur. Other colors of fur give this pupa year-round effectiveness: dark cream, brown, olive, tan, and yellow. This design has worked well across the country.

Top right: Humphreys Sulphur Nymph. Again I had to find out what a true sulphur nymph looked like. I picked up the rocks from the stream bottom and then watched the swimming, wiggling, rocking, pulsating action of the nymph in the water. That was the stimulus for this tie. I use brass wire for the light banding between the segments of the sulphur nymph's abdomen. The brass wire also helps flatten the nymph and gives it a rocking motion as the currents interplay over its broad surface. Light fur for the abdomen, dark fur spun loosely for the wing case, partridge wings on either side for motion, and a tail of partridge fibers.

Bottom left: George Harvey Stonefly Nymph. The George Harvey Stonefly has been effective from coast to coast wherever there are stoneflies. This flattened-body, two-toned nymph is tied by pulling three strands of chenille over a fur-dubbed body, ribbing with brass wire, and flattening with pliers. The flattened body, the partridge wings and tail fibers give the nymph motion.

Bottom center: Humphreys Cress Bug. The cress bug is a major food source in many limestone streams. The first trout I took on a nymph in the 1940s was with this imitation. I simply wrapped dark rabbit fur around the hook. Years later I realized the importance of the natural movement of the legs and the flat form. The real cress bug rocks in the currents and the legs move on the drift. So I blended a combination of brown seal fur, grey squirrel body fur, and muskrat. I spun the fur loosely, tied in a grisly hackle tip at the bend of the hook, palmered the hackle over the fur, and clipped and flattened the top. Then I added flex cement to the top of the flattened surface. Flex cement is good because it stays on top of the dubbing and doesn't soak in. It can also be colored by adding dye.

Bottom right: Humphreys Isonychia (bicolor) Nymph: This nymph pops up often on steams through the year. Its prevalence makes the fly effective. Because the nymph is a swimmer with lots of motion, use a tail of dark brown fibers or a few marabou fibers to give motion in the water. Extra motion is important. The body is black mink fur with a hint of brown, wrapped through black-dyed emu fibers for the gills. Tie in black-dyed gosling fibers and pull up and over two dark brown hackles intermixed on the front third of the hook and wrapped over the fur. When these nymphs are moving, this is a good one.

Cast in under those limbs and brush. It's the wrist, it's a very short stroke, the shorter the stroke—when you've got weight on—the better your chance of going in under the limb. On the forward stroke you let that rod tip drift to the level of or just below the limb, then *squeeze* off that short little powerstroke. It's no more than a squeeze. Thumb down, the thumb turns the leader over. The thumb is vital when you're working a pair of nymphs. You bring that rod *straight* forward on the forecast, not drifting the tip off to the right or left, then you check it—but if you don't push that thumb into it to turn that leader over, you'll throw a tailing loop—your nymphs will tangle.

Work right on up the stream making the changes you know you have to make, doing the work you know you have to do. When you see the bottom shallows up, take the time to pull your weights back up that tippet—straighten that cast out: tip drifts further forward before the check . . . go to a slightly lighter nymph, adjust your weights accordingly, go to 5X for that shallower water, pull your weights up, take one off, fire those nymphs right up tight along the shore, move on up, now it's in deeper water, now my nymphs are coming back to me too fast, so I stop and adjust, I pull my weight down toward my fly, add a weight maybe, drive the nymph in at a sharper angle, pick it up, follow it with the tip. If the nymph hangs up immediately that tells you it sank too fast (and may have gotten some debris on it). Make the adjustment.

Weight, position of weight, and leader diameter aren't the only tools to get a longer drift in deep water. You can cut your wrist off the tuck cast, cut a little hook upstream and mend to give your nymph more time on the bottom, to get a more extended drift through deep, swift current. You may be sacrificing a bit of line control through to your fly, but that may be a compromise you're willing to make. Or you can make the basic tuck cast and as the nymph tucks under and is heading into the water lift the rod upstream, lifting your line upstream and creating slack line on the water upstream of where your nymph has sunk to give you a chance at a nice long drift through water that's deep and fast. Again, you may have to give up some control—action, reaction . . .

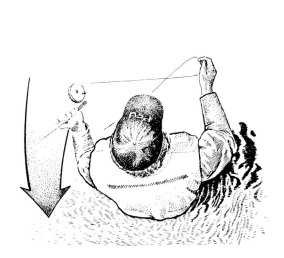

You bring that rod *straight* forward on the forecast—don't let the reel cant to the inside of your wrist; otherwise your line will cowtail and your nymphs tangle.

Nymphing at night.

Books have been written on night fishing. It's a thrill. The most explosive rises I have ever heard, the sound of them making the hair stand on the back of my neck, have not been for the dry fly or the nymph or the streamer . . . those sudden explosions are big fish—giants—chasing to take other fish in the night.

Few people nymph after dark because they think they can't see the take or they believe the trout can't see. But even on the darkest night if you have a good visible line 90 percent of the time you can see the end of the line. You'd be amazed at the line control you can maintain just by watching the end of the line. At night trout take much more decisively. They're really onto their feed—they've lost their inhibitions. When you see that line stop, you've probably got a fish.

Trout have excellent vision underwater at night. You can take them on a #12 or a #14 nymph under the water—I've done it hundreds of times.

I covered night fishing in depth in my first book, but there's one good tip I want to give you here: While the hatch is on you can take fish on the bottom with nymphs . . . and after the hatch is over you can *still* take fish with a nymph!

The night hatch is on. Lots of surface feeding.

But with the right nymph . . .

. . . I can catch fish.

Watch. The hatch is tapering off . . . I pump a modified tuck . . .

. . . as the nymphs come back I have good line control—I'm watching the end of the line . . .

. . . bang. The hatch has ended—the air's empty, but down under the water . . .

. . . they're still feeding on nymphs.

You can see why I feel that nymphing . . .

. . . can catch more fish in more situations, day and night, than most other techniques. *Night photos by Katharine Holsworth.*

LET'S TALK ABOUT LEADER AND LINE. LEADER DESIGNS ARE BASED on the type of fishing you want to do and the conditions you're about to face.

Leader lengths depend on several factors: water clarity and how close you can get to those fish, the depth and speed of the water, whether the water's flat or broken, your casting freedom, your ability to cast and control the leader, the elements (wind), your visibility—can you see the end of a long leader—the distance between you and your quarry, and the need for leader control.

What are the conditions you're facing? If I'm fishing a dryfly and have a great expanse of water with major intermixing currents and plenty of casting freedom, I'll use a longer leader. But on the very same water if I'm working the bank with brush and overhangs, I'll shorten the leader and adjust the tippet for

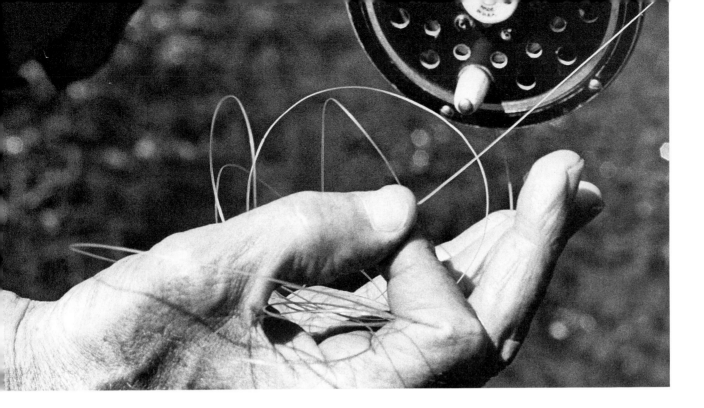

control and to get under the brush. If I'm working a small brushy stream, a leader of five to six feet may be the ticket.

With flat, low, clear water, I'll go with a longer leader. In broken water or pocket water I'll shorten the leader. When you're fishing a dryfly, leaders of twelve feet or more can be extremely difficult to control. They're difficult under any conditions and wind can raise hell with control and accuracy.

You've got to adjust tippet length as well as leader length. The tippet is proportioned directly to the density of the fly you're fishing—if you have a heavy air-resistant fly, you may have to shorten the tippet or go to a heavier diameter. What you're looking for when you cast are those soft "S" curves of leader up to the fly. If you're fishing a small fly, a midge, you might have to lengthen the tippet or go to a smaller diameter, or both.

If you're working across currents on open water or working heavy pocket water, you might want to lengthen the tippet. If you're trying to get under brush, shorten it, because a tippet that's too long will lift the fly over the brush, not under it, no matter how short the casting stroke.

When nymphing, the speed, depth, and clarity of the water are your guides. If the water is clear or deep, use a longer leader. In heavy broken water or off-color water, you may shorten the leader.

The tippet is also a consideration when nymphing in deep, fast water. A longer tippet with a smaller diameter can get you to the bottom. With currents pulling through the tippet, a tippet diameter that's too heavy and a tippet that is too short will pull the nymphs off the bottom or pull them at an unnatural speed.

When sight fishing in clear water, a longer tippet and a smaller diameter might be the answer. But for pinpoint control, don't make it too long. If I'm facing deep, heavy, fast water, I'll go to all mono for the line and taper the leader off the monofilament. With less diameter for the line, a lighter leader, and an extended light tippet (3X to 4X), I can roll the bottom slowly with great control and give my nymphs time on the bottom.

You must be flexible—there is no set formula. You must adjust to the conditions.

Some people advocate a 17-foot leader. They state, ''I use a 17-foot leader, period.'' Had I used a 19- or a 17-foot leader in some of these stream situations I've been showing you, I would have been into everything but fish. I would have had neither line nor leader control, nor control of the nymph itself. The adjustment of the basic leader is crucial. A lot of people advocate coming off the fly line with .023 or .021, simply to get the leader to turn over. But if you do this, by the time you construct the tapered leader—by the time you get out to the business end—your leader's going to be too long to handle.

In casting situations where I have to make short concise strokes to turn the leader over I come off the fly line with .017 (sometimes in dry-fly fishing I'll come off with .015). Believe me, it works. Your thumb will turn it over. That precise squeezing stroke as you push your thumb into the cast will turn the leader over beautifully.

It doesn't take more than 12 inches to come off the fly line. I'll fish with 10 inches off the line if I'm fishing a dry fly and facing a lot of tough casting situations—around trees, whatever. If I'm fishing nymphs, I might come off the line with 20 inches of stiff mono.

Tippet adjustment is crucial too, as I've said. You've got to regulate the tippet of the leader relative to the depth and the speed of the water. When I'm going into inches of water I may lengthen the leader and extend the tippet. I've got to get that distance. And I'm going to get a better sink rate if I change

diameters, go to a finer-diameter leader and tippet. In clear water on a clear spring creek sometimes it behooves you to go all the way to 6X, but I'd never go finer. You don't need it with a nymph. In fact, in most cases you really don't need to go as far as 6X.

So what I'm saying is that the diameter of the leader is directly related to the sink rate of the nymph. The smaller the diameter the deeper your nymph will sink. Once you combine diameter with sink rate of the nymph you're in business.

Early in the season lots of times you get into heavy, deep water—early run-offs—spring run-offs, and then you usually don't have to go below 2X, 3X, or 4X. Adjust the leader, adjust the tippet so it will get you down there.

When it's early in the season and I've got heavy run-off, I'll go to all mono; all mono and adjust and taper the leader off 20-pound-test Cortland or 20-pound-test flat mono. Flat mono doesn't have near the ordinary memory—it's soft and pliable and casts beautifully. And you have very little diameter, very little resistance, you get an incredible sink rate. So with your nymph—depending on how much you adjust the weight—you're going to roll the bottom in deep, heavy, fast water you could never touch otherwise. Early-season heavy currents push through a floating line that will belly and pull the nymph out of the productive areas. Conventional sinking lines and sinking tips are difficult to work in a stream. They belly, drag, and you have trouble with line control; you have limited control from rod tip to nymph.

Sometimes a conventional all-sinking line or a sinking tip is effective in a lake or a pond or slow water where you might want to work the bottom. If you're trying to take big cruising browns coming in out of say, Lake Ontario, and you're up to your ears in water; then you might double-haul and shoot a whole sinking line or a shooting head. Let it lay down on the bottom and start to work it back if they're down at that depth. But trying to work an all-sinking line or a sinking tip with good control while nymphing streams and rivers can be a problem.

It may work on a downstream approach. But if you're working upstream you just do not have the feel and control from nymph to rod tip. The sinking line or sinking tip creates a belly, and it's tough to get around it. On a downstream situation in a big river I'd rather put on a section of lead-core line. Tie it right into the leader and come off the leader with a short piece of mono and then your nymph. You can even put a nymph above the lead core. This way you can get distance—with a floating line—and you can lengthen the leader and get a heck of a nice bottom roll on a downstream approach. The weight is centered where it's got to be, not halfway between rod tip and nymph but down at the business end. The same system works with all mono as the flyline.

The trouble with all-lead-core lines is that you don't have the sensitivity, the feeling, the touch. You have a dragging situation.

Now in super-heavy water and awesome deep guts, a lead core sinking line's all right. The trout in water like this are not nearly as sophisticated—most of the time they don't have time to make a decision. They grab the nymph. The line stops and you set the hook.

But even on the Madison, or any water where fish have been fished over, they can be subtle, even in super-heavy water where they don't have a lot of time to make a decision. They can pick that nymph up and drop it just like lightning. And that's why I say mono for deep, heavy, fast stuff. It's better than any other technique I've used or seen.

PICK UP A ROCK. SEE WHAT'S LIVING ON THE UNDERSIDE. GATHER A handful of that lush aquatic vegetation and sort through it, see what's there. Keep experimenting to try and improve your imitation. In my book *Trout Tactics* I tie the Cress Bug. Since that book was published I've added a step—with flex cement you can put a shell on the fly. I tried to do this years ago but any cement I put on top ran through into the dubbing and made the nymph hard. Flex cement won't penetrate so I can put a case on top, and I have a lifelike imitation. It's hard on top, like the real article, and then it has the movement on the bottom. The other thing that a hard top does is keep the nymph flat. The nymph has a good flat shape that gives you a nice rocking and bouncing motion over the bottom. The interplay of the currents over the flat surface of the nymph gives it a rocking motion.

As I said in *Trout Tactics*, regardless what form of underwater life your nymph is trying to imitate, there's one basic essential it has to have—movement. You tie, cast, and fish artificial nymphs to imitate the undulating, pulsating, surging, gill-waving movement of the real thing. These super-realistic-looking new nymphs tied with vinyl and plastic just cannot compete with old-fashioned fur and hair for movement under the water. Remember, it's not how the nymph looks to you that counts. It's how it looks to the trout.

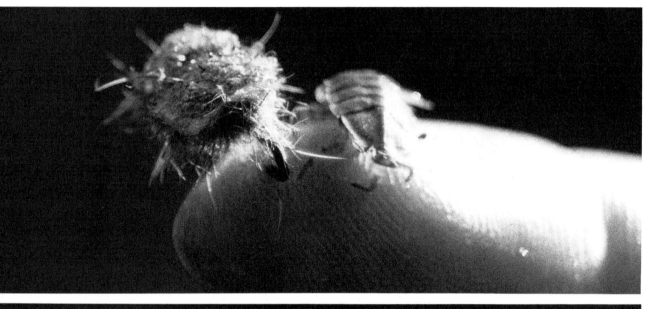

Dry Fly

IN THE DRY-FLY GAME REMEMBER, EVERYTHING YOU DO IS DIRECTED to get that fly drifting over the fish *without drag*. Every plan you plan, every move and adjustment you make—leader-construction, the cast that will complement the leader, and your approach—is done with that single end in mind: to get a natural, extended drag-free float. The way you get your drag-free float is to build your leader and present that leader with the correct cast to cause leader, and tippet, to come down on the water in loose coils, loose S-curves, all the way out to your fly. As the float begins, all those subtle, nearly invisible current changes will be absorbed by the leader and tippet to get the drag-free float you want.

When we talked about nymphing we talked about *lifting your line over as many current changes as possible,* and the dry-fly game is the same. Build that leader right, cast it so it comes down in nice soft S-curves. Lift your line over the current changes. The three basic factors in dry-fly fishing are: Build the leader and tippet section to complement the fly; make the cast that will complement the leader; position yourself for a drag-free float.

Here's what you attach the fly with *(right)*. I like a knot that reaches behind the eye of that fly and grabs it and locks it in position.

A lot of people say a clinch knot is as good as any but I want the fly to ride exactly the way I want it to ride, the way it was designed to ride. A turle knot sits behind the eye of the fly and locks behind the eye of the fly and keeps it steady so it doesn't turn over. The trouble with the clinch knot is that the fly will turn at different angles, and that's exactly what I don't want. So I reach up and catch the fly, pull it out in front, and bring that knot down. What I want to do is take this knot and drop it right over the eye of the fly. The Harvey Knot is also one that will accomplish the same end. *(See next page.)*

Whether you want an up eye or a down eye depends on the shank. With a longer shank you may want a down eye. With a shorter shank an up eye may be better. In both cases you're looking for the maximum amount of hook gap, for maximum hooking power. I've always felt a down eye on a short shank cuts off a lot of your hooking power. Divides the gap of the hook. You don't have quite the same power—unless the bend is off-set, kirbed, or reversed.

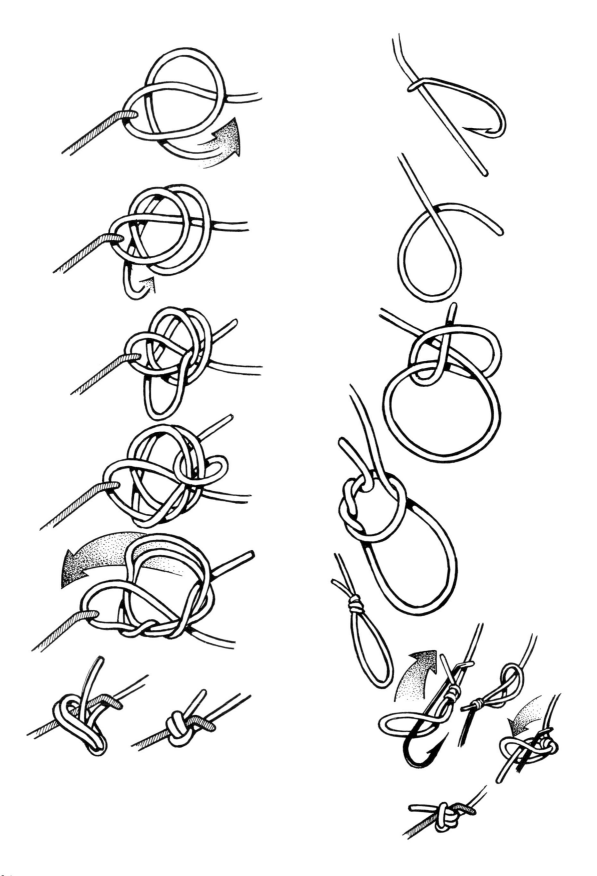

Leader

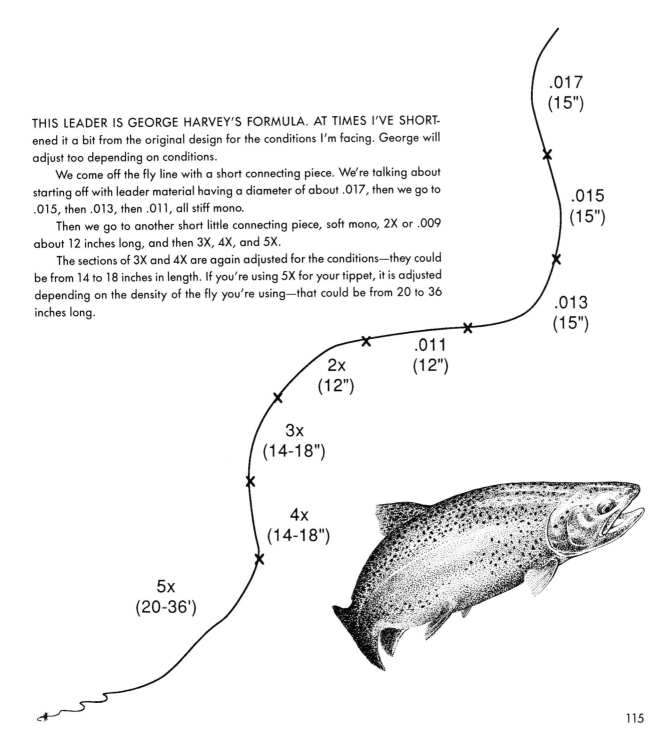

THIS LEADER IS GEORGE HARVEY'S FORMULA. AT TIMES I'VE SHORT-
ened it a bit from the original design for the conditions I'm facing. George will
adjust too depending on conditions.

We come off the fly line with a short connecting piece. We're talking about
starting off with leader material having a diameter of about .017, then we go to
.015, then .013, then .011, all stiff mono.

Then we go to another short little connecting piece, soft mono, 2X or .009
about 12 inches long, and then 3X, 4X, and 5X.

The sections of 3X and 4X are again adjusted for the conditions—they could
be from 14 to 18 inches in length. If you're using 5X for your tippet, it is adjusted
depending on the density of the fly you're using—that could be from 20 to 36
inches long.

.017
(15")

.015
(15")

.013
(15")

.011
(12")

2x
(12")

3x
(14-18")

4x
(14-18")

5x
(20-36')

LEADER CONSTRUCTION IS CRUCIAL. THE GEORGE HARVEY LEADER IS probably one of the more important developments in fly fishing in the last half century, and George took the time and had the patience to sit down and explain it to me, to work with me on it. It certainly has changed my success ratio by 150 percent.

The whole point in the dry-fly game—I really hammer away at this—is to get S-curves forming in your leader up to the fly *(see following two pages)*. You can have the best Snake Cast or Lazy-S Cast in the world and get all those nice curves in your line to compensate for the different currents between you and your float but if your tippet is straight you'll be dragging the minute your fly touches water. This can be subtle—leader and tippet drag isn't always something you see—but the trout can and it cuts your odds in half. You want the curves forming in your leader's soft forward section, and while the subtleties of the current are gradually straightening out all those leader curves, your fly is still getting a natural, drag-free float.

So here's a super-important point: Before I fish a leader I'll test-cast it until I can see I'm getting the lazy S-curve in the leader right up to the fly. Each fly has a different density. If my fly is so dense my leader folds back on itself, in other words I can't turn it over, then I don't have casting control. Then okay, I'll have to shorten my tippet or go to a heavier diameter.

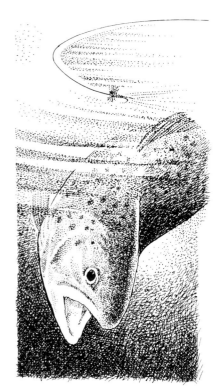

If I have a smaller or a less dense fly and I turn it over and my leader straightens out completely, then I'll adjust my tippet again. I'll lengthen my tippet.

Sometimes I start with an exceptionally long piece of tippet, simply because it's easier to shorten than lengthen. It's tough to lengthen a single strand of leader—it doesn't stretch. Am I going to get those S-curves? If I don't, okay, I will lengthen. Break the whole damn thing off and start again. If I'm not going to get what I need with it, if it falls back on itself, if it won't turn over, if I can't get the check with it, I'll take the fly off and do whatever I have to do to adjust. I might make two or three changes until I get exactly what I want. Just keep casting and adjusting the leader until it's right. That short piece of .009 is acting like a hinge. Your soft section is collapsing and dropping onto the current in those S-curves that get you that extended drag-free float.

And always be ready to adjust. Talking about nymphing we said *adjust your rig to get that point nymph down on the bottom.* Fishing a dry fly on the surface it's: *Adjust your leader so it will collapse into S-curves right out to the fly.* You have to be flexible. In wide-open water a longer rod and maybe a 9½ or a 10-foot leader will get you that extended float time. Move in tight to a brushy shoreline and you might want to cut each section down, shorten that tippet so it doesn't open up so much. Now you can punch that fly in under branches and other shore obstructions because no matter how tight your loop is, a tippet that's too long will lift that fly into the brush, not under it.

Build and rebuild, each time. If you're going into a brush situation along a small tight mountain stream, stop. Rebuild the leader and maybe cut back to 6 feet . . . if you come to a stretch where the forest opens up, stop. Tie a longer leader back on. Always adjust the leader and tippet to the stream conditions you're facing. Also adjust the tippet to the density of your fly. Yes it cuts into your fishing time to do this, but it can help you catch more fish, and *bigger* ones in the long run.

116

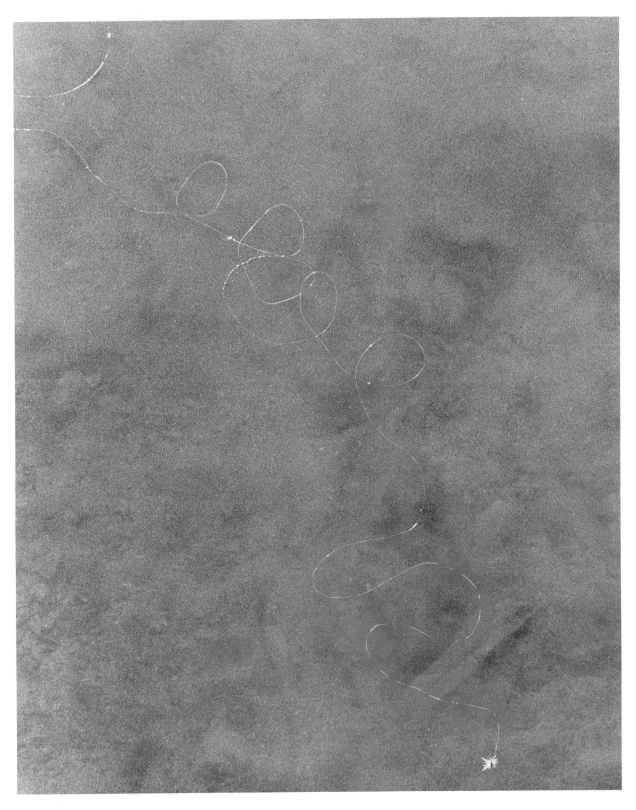

You want this, soft S-curves in your leader and tippet, right out to your fly . . . in the above photo there could be even more of an S-curve pattern in the six inches of tippet next to the fly.

And one more thing, use a *nail knot* to tie that leader to that line—don't fall back on loops. Thirty or more years ago we got away from loops. The reason we got away from loops is that we found that loops did numerous things—none of them good. With a loop at the end of your fly line, you've got bulk. You've got drag. I don't care about your casting stroke. No matter what you do, the more bulk you have in an area, the more susceptible you are to drag.

And if you should make a casting error, a tailing loop, your fly will hook on the leader-to-leader loops. In nymphing, if you loop your droppers onto the line, it's even more likely to happen.

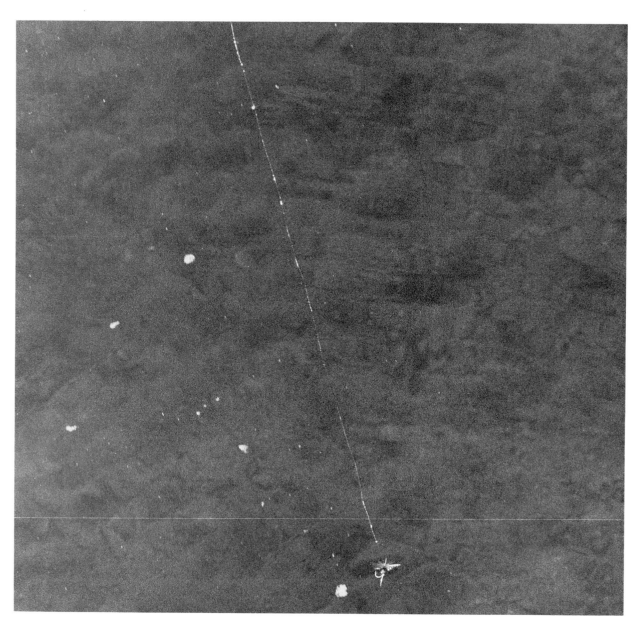

Not this. No matter how much slack I cast into my line, if I don't cast any slack into my leader and tippet I'm getting that subtle drag almost immediately.

The Cast

Here's the basic dryfly cast in brief. Lift as much line up off the water as you can, start it moving and then kick the wrist up with the thumb pointing up for the backcast.

Your line extends

out behind you. The wrist of the rod hand breaks slightly as your rod hand drifts forward

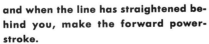

and when the line has straightened behind you, make the forward power-stroke.

119

Tap, stop the rod sharply and high, thumb pressing forward and third and fourth fingers squeezing back—the check,

and as the line travels out before you

"change levels," drop the elbow and casting hand

and lower

the rod tip, taking energy out of the line to collapse your leader and tippet in S-curves on the water.

120

LET'S LOOK AT IT AGAIN. YOU'VE CONSTRUCTED YOUR LEADER AND now you want the best cast to deliver your leader and tippet to the currents in soft S-curves. To achieve this you're going to check on the forecast (stop your rod high). As your loop turns over, you drop your elbow, then drop your rod tip—check, *bam, bam*, two level changes, elbow and rod tip.

"Changing levels" is important. You're lowering the level of the line by checking then dropping first your elbow and then your rod tip as the forecast is completing itself. This takes energy out of the cast—the "message" travels through the line and collapses the leader and soft mono and tippet on the water in the nice, soft S-curves you want.

The two photos at right start the basic dryfly cast. Start slowly, in low gear. Lift as much line off the water as possible before you make the backstroke. Get the line moving. Then make the backstroke, *lift*—it's a short *tap* with the thumb lifting skyward. The rod hand is in front of you and stops straight up. The wrist of the rod hand breaks slightly on the forward drift as the line continues to straighten out behind you . . .

. . . drift that rod forward with wrist and thumb pressing forward . . .

. . . then make the forward stroke and check it with a short, sharp *tap*. Stop that wrist and squeeze that thumb forward with downward pressure. This takes the line over the rod tip and helps prevent tailing loops. Rod unloads forward and throws line forward in the vertical plane. My non-casting hand is exerting line control at all times. Note that my casting hand and wrist are basically the only parts of me that have moved. In review, I drift forward on the forecast and check—stop the rod high. It's all wrist, wrist and thumb and last two fingers. Thumb presses forward, last two fingers squeeze back in toward me. Thumb stays on top of that rod handle, stays in the vertical plane, guiding and controlling the rod. I stop the rod—action—it unloads, sending that line out smoothly in the vertical plane—reaction. Now. If I stopped right here and just let the rest of the cast unfold, my leader would straighten out and it would be dragging the instant it hit . . .

. . . so I change levels. I'm going to lower through two levels—elbow drops, rod tip drops—to take some of the energy out of the line. I've lifted my line up off the water and kicked that wrist and accelerated that line back in the vertical plane of the cast back out over my shoulder, drifted forward, accelerated, given it the check, the *tap*, and now, as my line's straightening out in front of me I drop the elbow. I drop the elbow (compare position here to position on previous page)— first level-change . . .

. . . and I drop the rod and tip—second level-change. The energy's gone out of the line. My leader has received the "message" of the check and drop and drop and has de-energized and is about to collapse and lie down on the current in those soft coils and S-curves that will get me my drag-free presentation. Look how straight the latter part of my line is. That's all right because where I want slack is in my leader and tippet. I want that leader to turn over, but then the soft mono section must collapse, de-energize, and come down on those subtle current-changes nice and loose.

Here it is in a shot from a different cast-sequence: same thing. I've checked the forecast and *dropped* my elbow and *dropped* the rod tip and that message of de-energization has traveled right out through my line. My leader—the soft-mono section especially—has lost energy and will collapse on the water. I've been asked if all those coils and S-curves don't bother a fish—won't the fish see all that leader? It doesn't bother them—it doesn't bother them any more than a floating leaf bothers them. The crucial point, the point always to focus on in this dry-fly game, is that fish don't react so much to *what* is floating over them as they react to *how it is floating*. As long as those loose coils are drifting naturally the fish don't care—what spooks them is drag, a fly that's floating unnaturally.

Coming through on the forecast it's *check* (stop the rod sharply) . . .

. . . *drop* (down goes my elbow) . . .

. . . and *drop* (rod lowers). Also look how I've pulled my elbow back a touch, even further de-energizing that line.

THE PARTS OF YOUR CASTING HAND THAT DO THE JOB ARE THE thumb and the last two fingers. Your first and second fingers are just along for the ride. That thumb directs the cast and squeezes off the check. The thumb, by pressing forward and down, will turn your line and leader over. The interplay of thumb and fingers on the rod handle is a little like playing a guitar: thumb strokes down, third and last fingers pull up—back in, toward you. Try it. It's a kind of a leveraging and it has a hundred variations depending on what you want your rod and line to do. Those last two fingers are exerting a different pressure on the rod all the time. Sometimes they're relaxed, your whole hand and wrist are relaxed. Other times you're squeezing hard.

Turn back a page and look at my thumb and last two fingers in the top photo. I'm making the check on the forecast—look how that thumb is laying right on top of the rod handle, pointing in the direction of my cast, moving right through the vertical plane of the cast, controlling the check, making that forward *push* on the *tap*. See how relaxed my first two fingers are. Look at how my last two fingers are simultaneously squeezing back—in and under—to complement the forward push of the thumb.

ONE MORE NOTE ON THE BASIC DRY-FLY CAST; THEN I WANT TO review.

I've talked about the vertical plane of the forward cast and that's right. You want to do it as shown below, making a little circle with your casting hand on the backcast, as George's drawings show. If you came *dead* straight back and brought it *dead* straight forward you'd have a tailing loop; the line would kick on itself or hang on the rod tip; you could be throwing knots in your line. Downward pressure of the thumb on the forward casting stroke takes the line over the rod tip—and you avoid a tailing loop.

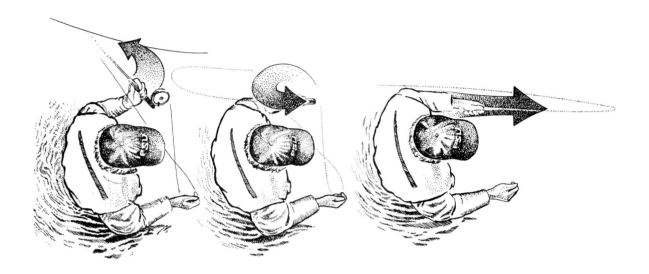

Here it is again. Lift as much line off the water as you can before you make the backcast. When you've lifted as much line off the water as you can, your line makes an angle to the water. Now, "climb the angle." In other words on the backcast take your rod tip . . .

. . . right up along the angle of the line. This is a tip my good friend Ralph Dougherty taught me. Chase the loop with the rod tip 'til the rod passes vertical. Stop the hand—*tap* . . .

. . . start the drift forward *(above)* having made the little circle we discussed, and check it *(immediately below)*, with that *tap*, squeeze. Thumb pushes into it/last 2 fingers pull back: *tap*. The rod unloads and the line unfolds nice and high. I'm starting to make the level changes in the photo at bottom: my elbow—you can see—has started to drop—level-change number one . . .

. . . and *bam, bam,* drop elbow drop rod tip. I've made the two level-changes quickly here—maybe I'm facing a lot of current changes and I want really to de-energize that line and collapse my leader and tippet and get a lot of good slack right up to my fly.

SURE, CHOICE OF FLY IS IMPORTANT, BUT IF YOU DON'T HAVE YOUR leader built right and you don't have the right cast to complement that leader, it can make a difference. Sometimes a dragging fly will take a fish—when fishing skaters or variants you employ drag. At times when mayfly duns are struggling for takeoff, a bouncing, dragging technique is productive. At the edge of darkness and into darkness, when a hatch first breaks and the duns are struggling for takeoff, sometimes I'll drag the fly intentionally, make the check and keep my hand and arm high—no level-change—dragging the fly right away so it skitters across the surface. But generally you're not going to do the job if that fly is dragging. Trout watch food come over them daily. They're in position—they might be there for hours. They know every little velocity change and subtlety by heart, and if your fly comes over them going at an unnatural speed, your chances of catching a fish are minimal. Lots of times your drag is imperceptible to you. But it's not to the trout. How many times have you watched a trout come up, stop at the fly, and drift right back down again? How many times have you watched a trout come up, watch your fly, drift with it, and bolt? You never see him again. Not only that, he screwed up the other trout in the pool. Well, you had a lousy float. You thought it was great, but the fish didn't. So take the time and make the effort to get that leader built right, and then learn how to cast so that whatever the stream situation you can get your leader and tippet coming down in loose coils right up to your fly; that will absorb the current while your dry fly's floating along like a natural.

Casting is a lot like shooting pool. In shooting pool you get all kinds of combos. You get bank shots, you get shots off the cushion, you get shots off the cushion hitting another ball.

Depending on where I want my fly to go and how I want my leader and line to float after it gets there, there's lots I can do.

If I'm standing in mid-stream and casting to much slower current in tight to the bank for example, and I've got to cast out over some really fast-flowing water and a lot of current changes to get my fly in tight to that bank, I might want to put a combo together to get a whole lot of slack in my line as *well* as my leader and tippet. I might want to: 1. Push my thumb up into the forecast to open a wide loop, 2. Cut my wrist to throw a hook in the line with an upstream mend, and 3. Change levels.

Here it is . . .

Right when I squeeze off the forward cast, as the line is coming forward . . .

. . . I throw a loop, or a hook, with the rod tip. Two ways to do this are shown in George's fine line drawings below. Then, changing levels, I drop the elbow and . . .

. . . bring my hand back into the normal casting plane, which enhances the loop
. . . the loop is now collapsing and my leader's beginning to stack.

I drop the rod tip . . .

. . . and line and leader collapse, giving me an upstream loop in my line with plenty of S-curves *right up to the fly.*

Here's that basic dry-fly cast one more time. It's power forward and . . .

. . . check it . . .

. . . drop it . . .

. . . and drop it. Note I've pulled my elbow back, in addition to changing levels, giving that line a real shock for maximum collapse.

More Casts

WHEN YOU'RE CASTING TO FAST POCKET WATER YOU WANT THE absolute maximum collapse you can get. You're going into the velocity change between two fast, broiling currents and you want to load the leader with ultimate slack. So to get maximum collapse you're going to drop both levels—elbow and rod tip—at the same time. You're *slamming* that elbow down and *driving* that rod tip down. Pulling the elbow back too. You do it all at once—bam—piling slack in that leader instantly. You're going back into the pocket and you want that natural float for as long as you can get it so you pile the leader up. It's not nice loose S-coils and curves right out to the fly; it's a dense *pile* of loops and curves. You can see my elbow and rod coming down together *bam*. I pull back, I pull my hand back, shocking that line further—look how my rod hand almost disappears as I pull it back in the lower photo. Look what's happening to that line. I pull that rod tip *down*, jamming that leader back. Then immediately I will lift as much line—with the rod—over as many currents as I can to give that leader and fly plenty of time to roll around in there.

If you need to punch your fly in under an obstruction here's a good way to do it. I lift my line off the water and kick it back—using just my wrist *(above photos)*. I've climbed the angle, taken the line back through the angle it made to the water when I lifted it off the water. I'm making a Circle Cast here, meaning I make an exaggerated circular motion as I pick that line up. My rod's tilted out away from me—it's not in the vertical plane—you can see the "circle" forming. Then *(photo below)* I bring that rod back to vertical—I bring the cast back into the vertical plane and I'm ready to start the forward drift . . .

. . . I drift it forward—here's the forecast—I accelerate . . . my thumb's pushing forward and down. The moment my rod tip is to the level of, or below, the obstruction . . .

. . . I squeeze off the powerstroke and stop the rod. It's a sharp motion with wrist and thumb . . . look how far forward I drifted that rod before squeezing off.

I've stopped that rod tip and my line and leader are shooting back in under the obstruction, shooting the whole way back in under . . . I won't get quite the S-curves in my leader that I'd like—I might not get quite the drift time, but I'm getting back in under where the fish are.

Or you can make the Underhand Lift—
this is a modified sidearm cast . . . both
on the backcast and the forecast *the line
travels at a level below that of the rod
tip.* At the end of the forecast you kick
your wrist up—this shocks your leader
and fly and they flip up, then collapse
down—and you change levels: elbow
and rod-tip. A good cast if you want
extended float time under the brush, or
when working lip currents.

144

HERE'S ONE CAST I WANT TO STRESS. IT'S THE MEND-IN-THE-AIR, a very productive technique *if performed correctly*. But what people don't understand is that you have to collapse the leader—you have to change levels and get the loose S-curves in that leader right out to the fly—whether it's the in-the-air-mend or the basic cast.

Flyfishers talk about the Reach Cast . . . they say with the Reach Cast your arm goes upstream as your line's going downstream and you reach the line out to the side, away from those potentially dragging currents directly downstream of you *(see photos at right)*. But what I did was to straighten the leader out, kick all the slack out of it and straighten it out on the water. I reached my line out to the side and avoided some current changes, but I've destroyed the whole purpose of the cast by not changing levels and thus straightening the leader out—I'll be dragging the moment it hits.

So watch what I do . . .

RIGHT!! In the sequence beginning here and continuing on the following two pages you'll see it done right. Coming through on the forecast *(above)* I check it . . .

WRONG!! Above you see a beautiful Reach Cast . . . my arm sweeps out to the side and my line stays off any current changes that may be right out in front of me. But I haven't changed levels! I've straightened that leader right out to the fly and it's going to be dragging from the word go.

. . . my arm extends in the Reach . . .

. . . and now I change levels—*drop elbow (look at that leader starting to collapse!)*

. . . and *drop* rod tip.

I WORKED HARD BUILDING THAT LEADER TO DO WHAT IT'S SUPPOSED to—give me that natural float—so instead of just reaching, I *change levels* off the reach. Check it and make the reach and drop the elbow, drop the rod tip. Drift it forward then check it, then reach, level-change, level-change.

Approach

BEFORE I MAKE A CAST, EVEN ON WATER I'M FAMILIAR WITH, I'll TAKE the water temperature. Trout migrate to colder waters when the temperature begins to hold in the 70- to 72-degree range. The migration might be from one side of the stream to the other or it might be a considerable distance to a cold tributary or a spring hole.

I watched the temperature of a favorite limestone stream in Pennsylvania climb to the low 70s after an extended drought. This is a stream that has never been considered marginal (meaning it holds a trout population its entire length for the entire year). Had I relied only on past experience and not taken a temperature I would not have taken a fish, but I knew the spring holes and the cold seeps and found fish.

Trout need oxygen. Between 9 and 11 parts-per-million (PPM) is prime, at 8 PPM trout can still be caught, and at 7 PPM trout start to move. I did some research on the Pine Creek watershed in Potter County, Pennsylvania, and found that at 7.2 PPM the migration was in full swing. The major migration took place at night.

The metabolism of a trout is keyed to temperature and oxygen. As temperatures rise from the 30s to the high 50s and mid 60s the body tissues of a trout demand food, thus the fish feed actively and deplete the oxygen. Then feeding ceases.

The migration of trout in water with rising temperatures has three basic phases. First, to the deep holes, when the temperatures hit 70 degrees for the first time. The bottom of a deep hole can have a 3-degree lower temperature, even with the intermixing of the stream's flow. Remember water in a stream never stratifies. Lakes and dams can, not streams or rivers.

The trout will hold in deep water during the warmest portion of the day and move toward the riffs at the head of the pool to feed. That's where the greatest amount of oxygen is, and they will feed early in the morning, late in the evening, and during the night. The cooler evening, night, and early morning air temperatures drop the water temperature a few degrees. This temperature change induces feeding.

As air temperature continues to climb and hold, so do the water temperatures, and the trout move from the deep pools to spring holes, the mouths of cold water tributaries, and above the cut-off point in the parent stream, where the water is colder.

Trout will lie in the mouths of the tributaries until the first heavy rains raise water levels. Then the migration continues up the tribs. Not all trout move from the mouths of the cold tributaries. The mouths of the cold tribs are always hot spots throughout the summer. Late in the summer I'll walk the tribs and enjoy fine fishing. Not all tributary streams are cold, and you may have to walk to the headwaters of a tributary to find cold water and trout.

The optimum temperature range will be from 55 to 65 degrees with 60 to 61 degrees the best temperature.

In Pennsylvania and in many large freestone streams across the country, if the rivers are not tailrace waters, coming from beneath a dam at cold temperatures, it is likely that where the streams and rivers broaden in the valleys, warm air temperatures will induce migration. In all of Pennsylvania's big northern freestone streams—Kettle Creek, Pine Creek, Loyalsock, the Sinamahoning—warm air and water temperatures cause yearly migration of trout.

Here's a tip. If there is a trout stream you've always wanted to fish but you are unfamiliar with the water, take a water temperature at the warmest time of the day, say from noon to 2:00 P.M., and if the water temperature is 70 degrees or above, look for colder water. If you take a water temperature at 10:00 A.M. and it's 68 degrees, look for colder water, but if it's 68 degrees or cooler at 2:00 P.M., the stream probably holds trout.

If you forgot your thermometer, here are some commonsense rules:

If you see rising trout then you know water temperatures are acceptable, but if you can take only sunfish, fall fish, rock bass, small mouth bass, and other warm-water species that have warmer optimum feeding temperatures (70 degrees plus), look for colder water.

If you fish a stream that is stocked with brook trout or has a native population of brookies, and you've always been able to catch these fish and suddenly you can't find a brook trout, it could be they have migrated. Brook trout need colder water; their optimum is 58 degrees.

Finding trout in marginal waters means being able to locate the cold spots and in part means finding the springs and sources of cold water. Take a look at the topography—a spring can feed in underneath where draws and gaps in the mountains and hills intersect with the river or stream. Look for dry stream beds that intersect with the stream; in most cases the water is still running, only it's coming in underneath.

White sand and gravel can signify a spring. Watercress and duck weed are clues that cold water is entering a stream. Watercress thrives only in cold water. Major outcroppings of limestone, shale, and sandstone along a stream can be an indicator. Springs can flow from the base of these outcroppings.

Prospect, just wade, put on your swimsuit or old dungarees and a pair of sneakers and walk in the stream. You'll know when you hit a spring hole. It's a shocking experience.

If you suspect there is a spring located somewhere within a deep hole, take a temperature at the top of the hole. If it's coming in at 68 degrees and is leaving the hole at 66 degrees, that 2-degree difference can mean a sizable spring within. Tie a thermometer on your line and cover the bottom till you locate it. You can wager there are trout lying in tight to that spring flow.

In the winter when it's bitter cold—air temperatures are below 0 degrees— walk a stream. Where that cold air meets the warmer temperatures of a spring,

vapor or steam will rise from that point. I've watched vapor rise from a spring hole as if it were smoke from a campfire. A walk in the winter can help you find a spring hole you've always wanted to find.

Major spring holes are not only hot spots in the summer but in the winter also. Beds of bright green watercress are easy to spot in a snow-covered landscape; it's a sure giveaway for a spring, and not only do these weeds harbor cress bugs, shrimp, and sculpin, but the warmer temperatures of the springs mean the trout can be more active feeders.

If you're sight-fishing, watch the trout, watch what side the fish is feeding to. Trout will feed to one side or the other. The major currents could be bringing the food to that side, or the food could be dropping off the bank to that side. The vegetation along that side may be loaded with freshwater shrimp, Cress Bugs, or mayfly nymphs, and the trout is either digging for them in the vegetation or intercepting the nymphs on that side. The sun could be a factor: the trout can only see to one side, blinded by the sun on the other.

If you're making an approach to a trout in flat clear water, your first cast might be behind the fish. When it feels the vibration of the fly hitting the water and turns, the first thing the trout sees is the fly, not the leader.

If the first cast is up over the fish, even if you don't line the fish, the leader drifting by the fish can well put it down.

The second cast should be off to the side, at an angle to the fish. When the fish turns, it will see the fly, not the leader.

The third cast is above the fish (but not too far) and at an angle, so again the trout sees the fly first, not the leader. If the trout has too long a look at the fly it can refuse it. Lay the fly inches above the trout. Now the trout will have to make a quicker decision, and a short drift will help maintain a drag-free float—as long as the leader is built correctly and the cast did its job.

Always make the adjustment—if you're going to a much lighter fly take the time to tie on that longer tippet and vice versa—trim that tippet back if you're going to a more dense fly or if you have to punch a low, tight loop in under some branches.

Keep the slack out of the line that is in front of the rod tip. The whole way through the float, keep stripping the line in, smoothly—keep in touch with the fly. Off the cast immediately begin to strip in the line, don't let the slack build up. If your line starts to drift behind the rod tip—downstream of the rod tip—you're going to have a hard time trying to hook a fish if it takes because you'll have to pick up all that excess slack first.

But don't pick up so much line you pull the soft coils and S-curves out of your leader and tippet.

Avoid the heavy currents and current changes between you and the velocity change you're fishing. Lift up over those currents with that longer rod. Position yourself to cast around them. If you can't avoid them, make the cast that'll complement your leader to get the job done.

If you're facing a lip current—that difficult, swift tailing water at the tail of a pool, get off to the side and lower your profile and come in at an angle. Cast your line over a rock or the bank to lift and hold the line over the fast water if you can. The S-curves you pile into your leader will give you a good float of a few seconds as your fly floats down over the swift lip-current.

If you're not getting any action don't camp on it. Move on, try a different angle and float. Cover as much water as you can—the more fish you fish over the better your chances.

If you're not getting any action at all with a dry fly, go under with a nymph.

You try and think of all these things. Fish the velocity changes. Cast at an angle to the fish. Lead the fly with the rod tip. Don't let 'em see you. Lift your line over the current changes. Keep in close touch with the float. It isn't easy. You've got to keep at it, keep pounding away . . . I get pretty excited. When I retire I hope to have the time to really learn this great game. These were also the words of George Harvey who retired seventeen years ago. He had fished all his life but knew there was still more to learn.

Lip currents can be hell where the current converges, narrows, and races out of the tail of the pool. Drag is most difficult to overcome.

If the water is dropping a considerable distance over the lip, you can lower your profile and slide in behind and below the drop or falls. Check the cast; drop the elbow and rod tip quickly to stack the leader, then quickly elevate the rod with the full extension of the arm to lift as much line as possible over the lip and strip in the additional slack. Don't cast too far beyond the lip. The fast water pulling through the line will straighten the leader and immediate drag will occur. Drop the fly only a short distance above the lip; it's a short float.

If the lip is a shallow lip or if the drop between the lip and the base of the falls is too great, get an angle on it. In shallow lip currents, a solitary frightened fish can alarm the others and that pool is finished. One of the best strategies is to move off to the side, get an angle on the lip, and cast over a rock, boulder, the bank, or any object that will hold the line, and in part, the leader, off the water to enable the fly to float drag free.

Once you're into a trout in that fast funneling lip current, get it down out of there before it runs into the pool and spooks the others.

Get an angle on the lip current.

Throw your line over an obstruction, a rock or log—the obstruction will help hold as much line as possible off the currents for a drag-free float.

Lift as much line as possible over the lip current.

Low-profile approach—don't let 'em see you. I've got the sun at my back, that sun coming over my shoulder at the fish. They can't see into the sun . . . they may be feeding to their side that's away from that direct sunlight. Notice I've moved upstream around that tailing lip current in the lefthand side of the photo . . . if I cast across, above that current, I've got a better shot at a drag-free drift.

Look for the feeder streams. Where the tribs tumble in there can be cold water, there's food, and there's fish, especially if the temperature of the main stream's been rising and the tribs are cold.

Get a handful of vegetation and see what you can discover crawling around in it—in addition to checking the water, the air, and the banks for insects. (Can you spot the nymph?)

Trout feed to one side or the other. The fish could be feeding away from the sunlight. Or feeding where the food's coming from. The current might be bringing food to the fish from that side. Or vegetation in tight to the bank might be producing food, such as cress bugs or nymphs. A rotting log might house carpenter ants that drop into the water. Watch the fish. When you've established which side he's feeding to, that's the side you want to work. If the water's flat, your first cast might be behind the fish *(right-hand arrow above)*. If the water's quiet enough he may feel the vibration from your fly touching down on the water and turn. If that cast doesn't take the fish, move up. Cast to his side, the side he's feeding to, as shown by the middle arrows. Cast to the fish from an angle, so he sees your fly first. If you cast up over him, or up alongside him, he'll see your leader. The leader can spook 'em. Cast from an angle. In the photo above the water's not flat enough to cast behind him, it's moving too fast, so I'd make my first cast to one side or the other *(middle arrows)* and only then go upstream of him *(arrows to the left)*. If he turns, give the fish time to inhale the fly before you set the hook. And don't cast the fly too far upstream of the fish—it gives them too long to look at it.

You can keep your line up over the currents by fishing with just leader. Drop the fly . . . into the open velocity changes in the stream vegetation and give it a quick float, get ready to lift.

Don't let 'em see you. If there is water clarity and their visibility's good, don't get close. Shoot for more distance—you can get a lot of line out with just the compact lift and *tap* for the backcast, drift and *tap* for the forward cast.

Sometimes the shallow pockets—we tend to skip them but there are fish there. They're laying in those pockets. Don't neglect shallow water . . . I've lowered my profile, approaching at an angle to the fish . . .

. . . I tighten and lift back as the trout inhales . . .

. . . I get a good side-angle on him and keep the fish off balance.

Fire that fly in under that obstruction . . . I make another circle cast, using just the wrist—only wrist and rod are moving.

While that line goes out behind you on the back cast *(above)*, drift it forward *(below)* and when the rod tip goes below the level of the obstruction you want to get under, squeeze off the stroke. Where your thumb and knuckles and rod tip are pointing, that's where the fly's going to go.

I've sent my fly way back in under the branches and right away I get in touch with my line and leader. I lift the tip and start to strip in the line coming back to me.

When that line's gone beyond—i.e. downstream of—my rod tip the float's usually over: I'm not in touch with it *(below)* and the fly's started to drag.

I'm making a downstream approach *(above)*. I've laid my line down over that boulder, keeping the line up off the water and up off those currents long enough to give me a better float. Also that boulder gives me a little concealment. In the photos to your right I'm getting a natural drift along the edge of a faster current *(top)*. Notice the loop in the line, indicating a velocity change. In the cast the hook was thrown in the tailing currents. By the time the faster currents dissolve the loop, I will have had an extended drag-free drift. In working the velocity change, I'm moving up, taking up excess slack in the line as the float comes back to me *(bottom)*. I've got that more-or-less 90-degree angle coming off the rod tip—you've got to have line control, even though you're throwing slack. You maintain control and pick the slack up as the float comes back to you. You can't get hypnotized by your fly and forget to stay with the line. If you lose track of that slack building as your upstream cast floats back to you, when the trout takes, you won't be ready.

164

If you make your approach at a good angle and keep all excess slack out of the float as your fly is drifting, you're halfway there to making a successful hook-up and getting the trout off balance as soon as it's hooked. I shorten the rod with my non-casting hand to give me extra leverage . . .

. . . I put side pressure on him, keeping him off balance. Look at the velocity change where I picked him up, right where that deeper water runs alongside the vegetation: change in water-color, change in depth, change in lightness and darkness of that water—velocity change. I had the sun at my back and that was to my advantage. They don't have eyebrows and lashes and eyelids and they can't see into the sun, and he was feeding to his left, away from me.

167

Don't let 'em see you. If I don't have to get into the water I'm not going to. Here's the rollcast out and across-stream, from the bank. I've kept away from the fish, I've stayed on the bank, but to do this I've got to cast a longer line and adjust for those subtle current changes, between me and the fish, that threaten drag. So I change the levels—it's crucial. Drop that elbow and drop the rod tip. *(See facing page.)* Down comes my elbow and down comes the rod tip. I've shocked it, I've de-energized it so my leader's not going to straighten out. The leader's going to collapse in a nice series of loose coils and S-curves. Even though I may have some subtle current changes pulling through my line, my leader and tippet will give me float time.

Big current change between me and where I want my fly. I've thrown a hook around that current change and now, as my float starts back to me . . .

. . . I lift my long rod to keep my line up over those currents between me and the velocity change I'm fishing. I've got the "90-degree" angle, I'm in touch with it. I've immediately crouched, lowering my profile—each step, each little thing, helps your chances. I could have fished this situation from a position directly downstream, but this way I've got a good angle on the fish.

We're fishing intermixing currents and pocket water with a dry fly. It's position and stream approach. Say a fish is breaking in there where I'm pointing . . .

. . . if I try to work it from this position, no matter how many curves I throw in my line and leader that heavy, fast current is going to deprive me of any kind of natural float . . .

. . . so I get close, I get as close as I can—lower that profile—use that long rod to lift. I get my line up over those currents. An 8-foot rod is good here, a longer rod even better. It's an across-and-downstream drift, my fly comes to the fish first . . .

. . . float's about over. The fly's going to start dragging but I got a good, natural float in along that bank. I really like the longer rod. This notion that 6½-footers and shorter are the epitome of brush or tight fly fishing is wrong. A smaller rod gives you some casting freedom and that's about it. You've got too much line on the water. It's hard to get a drag-free float with a short rod in a situation like this one.

Always make the adjustment. I need a longer leader and lighter tippet here for the less dense fly I'm going to use. I've seen a fish rising over by that far bank. Take your time, build the leader right and tie on the right tippet, the right length and diameter for the situation.

Now I make the cast. I've got the sun coming from behind me and I'm a good distance from that trout. I'm in control of the line through the cast. I'm casting to a specific spot—I've changed the level to get the leader-collapse I want, but not too much, it's not going to be an extended float—if he takes it's going to happen fast.

He inhales my fly and I start to tighten—I give him just that second to inhale, and strike. It's all wrist. Give it that lift and *tap*: set that hook.

Get an angle on him right away. Keep him off balance.

Holding my line in the same hand that's holding my rod I keep a good tight line on him while I'm reeling in slack.

Line control the whole way through. I'm paying attention to the fish . . . he's ready.

Concentrate—pay attention to what you're doing the whole way through the process of playing and releasing that fish. The rule *Never point your rod at the trout* applies right through playing and landing—you want to keep a good angle and side-pressure on the fish the whole way through. You've played him with a combination of stripping and using your reel and always using the rod. This process continues to the release. Striking, playing, and landing is hard to practice . . . you can practice tying knots and you can practice casting and you can practice approach whenever you like but to practice setting that hook and playing the fish you need the trout's cooperation.

The Mayfly Strategy

WHEN WORKING A MAYFLY HATCH, LET INSECT ACTIVITY BE YOUR guide. If you see just a couple of insects in the air or emerging from the surface, stay on the bottom with nymphs—work the pockets and velocity changes.

As the hatch progresses I'll stay on the bottom and work the tuck cast, the modified tuck, and the downer-and-upper till I see some surface activity from the trout. Then I'll work over those fish with unweighted nymphs, or nymphs tied with minimum weight and no weight on the leader, straightening the cast so I have immediate line control from rod tip to nymph.

In the late afternoon and evening hours into darkness, with heavy hatching activity the predominance of insects can be on the surface. Now a goodly percentage of the trout population will be feeding on top, and I'll go to the dry fly—*with flexibility*. If they refuse the upright wing, go to a spent-wing, low-profile floating fly—and pay attention to the size of the insect. Match size, shape, and silhouette the best you can.

Always be flexible—I'm constantly changing complete systems, from bottom to sub-surface to top and back to the bottom again, depending on insect activity or the lack of it, the trout's activity, and the water conditions I'm facing.

The three photo series that follow show how you can follow a hatch up from bottom to top. First *(right and on the following two pages)* I work the bottom with weighted nymphs at the outset of the sulphur hatch.

179

Fishing unweighted nymphs (with a bit of split shot on my leader) now, I pop a cast across the heavy currents into the velocity change on the far side. I saw a fish break on the edge of the heavy current; I'm betting the trout will take the nymph.

The drift was a short one. Seeing the trout swirl as it took the nymph, I set the hook.

The trout rolls in the current.

Side pressure keeps the fish off balance and . . .

. . . I change the angle . . .

. . . and reach for the fish.

I'm working upstream. The hatch is moving up, the nymphs moving up off the bottom. I've removed the weight from the leader, and with two unweighted nymphs I'm working the pockets, velocity changes, and the shallow edge of the current—my dropper is located about two feet above the tail nymph.

The trout have moved to the top. They're feeding on the sulphur emergers and duns as the mayflies surface.

I'm pointing to the area just under the limb, where a fish took a sulphur dun on top.

I can't take the fish from this position, though. The currents are too fast and heavy immediately in front of me.

I've got to position around as many currents as possible for a drag-free float.

I can't take that fish from here.

I've moved upstream, closer to the trout, and positioned myself to get around as many currents as possible—and at an angle to the fish.

I drift the rod forward and squeeze off the forward casting stroke to get the fly under the limb . . .

. . . and quickly elevate the rod tip to get the line and leader over the heavy current. A longer rod such as this nine-footer helps get as much line as possible off the water. The leader is constructed to give the fly float time in the productive area where the trout surfaced.

The trout sizes in the fly; I have good line control and set the hook.

The trout begins to tail-walk . . .

. . . and explodes back under the limb.

I pressure the trout from under the limb.

With side pressure I lead the fish to the velocity change below me, and change the angle again . . .

. . . keeping the pressure on and the fish off balance.

With back pressure from the palm of the hand

I lead the fish to me, and with thumb and forefinger grasp the fly.

Small Mountain Streams

BRUSH FISHING—PROSPECTING FOR TROUT IN NARROW, LOW-water, tree-and-brush-protected little streams in mid- and late-season—is the most exciting action there is. It's hard, taxing fishing but the thrill is incomparable when you take a big trout out of the head of a low, clear pool guarded by rhododendron and branches. Your leader's basically the same as the regular dry-fly leader, the same stiff-mono/soft-mono setup I described earlier, only it's much shorter. You're going to be looking at possibly five or six feet of leader, depending on how tight or open the stream is. I might come off the line with 11 inches of .017, then 9 inches of .015, 9 inches of .013, 10 inches of .011(0X), 9 inches of .009(2X), 9 inches of .008(3X), and 14 inches of .007(4X) out to a number-twelve Humpy. That's about six feet and it's tight but it's all I need—I'm going to have to shoot that leader up under branches and boughs and leaves and all kinds of low-hanging obstructions, and I'll want to keep the loop tight.

An understanding of trout, habits and habitat, in this case native mountain brook and brown trout, will help in catching them.

When mountain and brush streams reach their summertime low-water levels, the trout move and congregate in the pools because they have a greater surface area that harbors more food, plus depth and cover for safety.

Within these pools the trout establish a pecking order and line up as if they have been sifted or graded by size. This helps to insure the preservation of the species. The largest trout assumes a position where the major currents bring the most food to it and where there is cover nearby.

The smaller trout are on the other end of the order. If they weren't, they could very well end up on the inside of the dominant trout.

If water temperatures rise, the largest fish might take a position at the head of the pool, where broken water tumbles in and the greatest amount of oxygenated water is found. The largest fish needs more oxygen, thus my approach in this situation would be to deliver the first cast to the top of the pool, in tight to the broken water.

In most cases, however, the major currents sweep to the tail of a pool and bring the greatest amount of food to the lip of the pool; the best fish can be controlling this position. If I take a good fish at the tail, or off that lip current, I won't make another cast. I've taken the best fish. I'll go to the next pool. If I take a small fish at the tail of a pool, my next cast is further up into the pool or at the head of the pool.

But the pecking order is not necessarily from the top to the bottom of a pool, or bottom to top. It can be from one side to the other. If I drop a fly along the side of a pool in a velocity change, in some slack water, and take a parr-sized fish, my next cast will be in the major velocity change on the other side. Remember, wherever that little fellow is, the biggest trout is on the other end of the spectrum.

Your approach is not only dictated by the pecking order but by the physical aspects of the pool. An upstream approach is usually the most desirable because in most cases fish face into the currents and that is a great percentage of the time upstream, so you can usually position yourself behind the fish for the best advantage. It is more difficult for the fish to see you. But there are times when an upstream approach is impossible. Obstructions such as brush, limbs, rhododendron, can block an upstream approach. Then your approach is either off to the side of the pool or at the head or top.

To position from the top or side can be demanding. Trout can be alerted by the slightest movement. I've had trout scurry at a distance of 40 feet. Often a cast of considerable distance, laying the line over a great span of bank, is required or a casting approach where the water is not visible to the angler.

Before flyfishers can make a cast, they must consider casting freedom, whether they are right- or left-handed. Often a low-profile approach and the use of foliage to help break your outline is demanded. A low profile might mean a position on both knees in the water.

Distance casting and the ability to cast 40 feet of line in tight cover is one of the greatest challenges in all of flyfishing. It requires technique and the utmost concentration.

I remember one occasion when George Harvey and I were working a mountain freestone stream in Potter County, Pennsylvania. George saw a trout rise at the tail of a pool 50 to 60 feet ahead. George said, ''Drop down on your knee and make a cast from here.'' ''Let me get a little closer, George, so I can clear the tree behind me,'' I said. As I lifted to move the trout raced up through the pool and it was over. George's comment: ''Why didn't you take him from here? Can't you cast?'' Don't think fish can't see a considerable distance in that low, clear water.

I've heard flyfishermen talk about poking the rod through the brush and dappling the surface with a fly, but if you get that close in low, clear water conditions, those fish are gone. You might make this approach when there is a greater flow with more turbulence, or when you're out of sight of the water and employ a bow and arrow cast, or cast over the bank and remain out of sight. But wiggle that rod tip over open water in low clear conditions and your chances diminish. Movement spooks fish—movement means danger. Hang your fly on a limb with a bad cast, shake the limb to release your fly—and they're gone.

Once you've established position, consider what is behind you; where must the line and fly go on the backcast? Point your rod tip to the opening where the fly must go. Consider the rod angle, the length of the casting stroke, then computerize it in your head. Now concentrate on what is before you—what must you cast over and under, analyze the casting stroke, distance, and direction. You may have to go over a log and under a hemlock limb a foot above the water at a distance of 35 feet. You need total concentration on what is before you.

The theory has been pushed that you look back on the backcast in a tight

brush situation, and then as you make the forecast you look forward. But if you do this, by the time you look forward you've lost concentration and control, your fly will be into everything but the water, and distance and accuracy are impossible.

Now with the rod tip put the line in motion. You know where your backcast must go—it's in the memory bank. You have enough line in your non-casting hand for the distance you need. And remember you have control of the fly. Also, if you drop the fly before the rod tip is in motion, if there is anything for it to catch on it will. Make the circle with the rod tip, it's a circle cast you're going to make. The size of the circle is directly related to the space available. Once the circle is made and your line is in motion, release the fly—drift the rod forward and down to the level you want your fly to go below.

Squeeze—it's a very short forward casting stroke. The forward stroke and the push of the thumb is almost imperceptible. The squeeze with that short stroke not only gives you distance but tightens the loop and enables you to get under that limb.

Once the cast is made it is easier to obtain greater distance on the next cast. The water resistance will help not only in slipping out more line but in loading the rod tip for the next cast. You may find it easier to employ a circle roll cast for distance. It may be easier to find casting freedom for the rod tip off a roll cast. Remember if there is a limb directly in front of the rod, make sure the rod tip is in front of and beyond that limb before you make the cast—it is so easy to misjudge distance and rap the tip off a limb.

Don't false cast. Once the line and rod tip are moving shoot the cast; each cast is successive into the business district. With false casting the more you wave the rod tip back and forth the more you're hung up.

Keep the line and fly dressed. You don't need to false cast.

Another thing that I disagree with is the use of the short rod in the brush. So many people advocate the use of a short rod 6-foot to 6½-foot for a 4 or 5 weight line—the shorter the rod, the more casting freedom. That is fine in theory, but I want as long a rod as I can get away with. My preference is a 7-foot or a 7½-foot rod for a 6 weight line. Preferably a 7½-foot rod. If I have any freedom the longer rod can give me three definite advantages. I have more line control on the water. I can lift over more currents for a drag-free float. And the heavier the line the more it can load the rod in a shorter period of time, and that is one of the secrets of distance in the brush.

With a short rod you've got too much line on the water and you're constantly fighting for line control. You can't get an extended drag-free drift. And when you're facing tail currents or lip currents line control is nearly impossible. You can't lift enough line over the major currents for an extended drag-free float. With a short rod calling for a 4 or 5 weight line you can't load the rod tip in a short period of time. No matter what casting stroke you employ, you simply don't have the tools to do the job, not in low, clear water with movement-shy fish, where distance means success.

Holding in your non-casting hand the line you've stripped out—the amount of line that you're going to be casting . . .

. . . you look back, calculating how much room you have, programming in your mind the exact distance behind you that you're going to move the rod on the backcast, and the exact area you're going to do it in . . .

... then looking straight ahead you make the circle, you start that little counter-clockwise motion with your casting hand to get your line in motion and you release the fly and squeeze off the cast. (Note: the circle's counterclockwise for me because I'm a lefty. If you're right-handed make that "clockwise," from noon back around through to noon.)

Having programmed my mind with the exact cast I want to make, I hold the line and fly, having stripped off the amount I want to shoot . . .

. . . and make . . .

. . . the circle . . . and when I've got that line moving I squeeze the rod handle with that imperceptible forward stroke —and release the fly—for the forward cast . . .

. . . changing levels—drop elbow and rod tip.

200

I've got room to make a little roll. I'm fishing the productive area, the deeper, flat-surfaced water in tight to cover, just beyond the sunlight. That's a major current for such a tiny stream. Food is carried in along the bank and that's where they'll position. I lift my line—

—give it a short drift forward and *touch* it, stop it, and my line . . .

. . . rolls right up through. The stroke is so short in brush fishing, so quick. From the start to the finish of the cast the only thing I've moved is my wrist—the casting stroke is an imperceptible squeeze.

Stay back from the water! Cast from thirty, from forty feet—sound hard? You bet it's hard. You have to have control of your casting stroke and be concentrating every second . . . to retrieve my line up over the bank, debris, limbs, or any obstruction, I get the line in motion by moving the rod tip from side to side as I lift—helps keep my fly from hanging up.

Here it opens up—I've got some room—if it's more open they can be more wary, so I stay back, I shoot way upstream. Had I poked my rod out through the rhododendron like a lot of people tell you to do I would've spooked whatever fish might be up there in that broad, flat-surfaced holding water. So I position myself at a greater distance. Notice the forward drift and *tap* is wrist, all wrist and thumb . . .

. . . I've taken the time to lengthen my tippet for this more open water, and I've got the luxury now of being able to push my thumb up into that cast to open the loop and get real good collapse of leader and tippet for a drag-free float. I change levels *(above photo to below photo)* to help achieve this. When you're firing tight-looped casts through dense brush you're less able to open that loop, but if your leader's built right you can still get S-curves.

Skip the unproductive water—I've ignored the rocky shallow water and I'm shooting to the broad, flat surface I see above, a good holding pool. Only my wrist moves as I control that line with my non-casting hand *(top)*, make the circle with my wrist *(middle)*, and *tap* it (non-casting hand opens, releasing that shooting line, as I'm not going to a specific, localized patch of water) *(bottom)*. I've positioned toward the right side of the stream to give myself casting room—I'm a lefty remember—but if the situation called for it I'd position left and cast across-chest. I've laid my line out over the rocks in front of me and up along the rocks to the right of the pool *(arrows)* to give whatever fish might be there a good drag-free drift. The rocks are helping me. I've cast my line over the rocks to stay away from the very subtle lip current there at the tail of the pool. I've got an angle, and the rocks are holding my line off the water.

My first shot here is to the lower edge of the pool below that downed tree. Good flat holding water with a little depth. In most cases two casts are sufficient, unless the pool is a long one. If I make two good shots in a pool and nothing happens, I move . . .

. . . up to the next good water. That flat water running up through the alley of brush to the right looks promising—plenty of cover for them . . .

207

. . . and plenty of problems for me. I can't get the shot I want from here. I need to be able to get my rod out in front of those obstructions . . .

. . . so I move up until I can cast with my rod in front of those obstructions. I'm getting close to those fish now so I lower my profile, I make the circle, I drift forward, accelerating—

209

—and squeeze off the shot. I've laid my line out over the rocks in the right center of the photo to keep as much line off the water as possible, and I've been able to shoot good distance up in under that brush, up into that protected alley of flat water.

. . . and here's the result, a fine little brook trout took my Humpy. They're such a beautiful fish in the sunlight . . it always pays to take a moment to appreciate them, before you put them back in the stream. Stop and smell the flowers.

211

Here it is, here's the secret of fishing small streams—to be able to make that long low shot way the hell up to the head of that pool. I'm going to shoot forty feet here—in under all those low branches and up to that half-submerged little log on the left—good shelter for a big fish. Concentrating on where I'm going and how I'm going to get there I start to make the circle . . .

. . . only my wrist moves. I start the drift forward—it's gonna be fast when it comes, all wrist and hand, forward-and, forward-and . . .

. . . bam. My elbow tucks in and lowers—in a fraction of a second I've drifted the rod forward with my last two fingers pulling and my thumb pushing forward and down toward my target to turn that leader over fast and you can see my line—good tight loop—firing up that rhododendron alley. Right downstream of that log, about three feet downstream of where I want to cast, there's a branch hanging out about twenty inches above the water—I've got to get my leader under that branch, and that's why I'm working with just six feet of leader. I bring that rod down until the tip's below the level—in my line of sight—of the obstruction I want to shoot under, then I squeeze off. It's subtle, it's all *wrist and hand*, and *fast*.

I've gone in under that branch with a tight loop and now my Humpy's floating right by that log, a good hiding place. Do you think I could've made this shot with a six-foot bamboo rod and ten feet of leader and tippet? No way. I straighten my leader out a little more than I'd like on a shot like this, but that's unavoidable when you're firing in under the brush—and three feet beyond—a branch only twenty inches off the water. It's what you've got to do on these small streams— shoot it low, way up to the head of the long pools . . .

That's where you'll find them. This trout came shooting from under that log. I could see his wake as he came to the fly. Where the casting's hardest the water's most protected, and where the water's most protected the fish hang out. The more difficult the cover the less shy they are. But you can't get close. Stay well back and shoot thirty, forty feet up to 'em—you'd better have the brush-casting technique down before you try it. This fifteen-inch native brown (you can tell he's a native from the haloes around his spots) made the day, made all that toil worthwhile. I think small-stream fishing is my favorite, but you have to be in shape and you have to have your concentration at a high pitch.

Some Things To Remember

THE CAST IS A SHORT STROKE. WHETHER YOU'RE NYMPHING OR fishing a dry fly, whether you're casting for distance or short-lining it, whether you're working over wide-open water or casting in tight brush, *keep it short.*

In 90 percent of the casting involved in tactics for trout the short casting stroke is imperative *(below)*. A short stroke tightens the loop to get you under the brush. A short stroke in nymphing will give you the tuck cast; a short stroke gives you that good high check of the rod, and with the level changes of both elbow and rod tip, a dynamic float of the dry fly, if the leader construction is right. And even for distance the short stroke, with the double haul and without the use of extended arm motion, can tighten the loop and result in a distance cast into a heavy wind. A lot of arm motion *(right)* may look impressive, but if you want more success on the stream, the short casting stroke is the key.

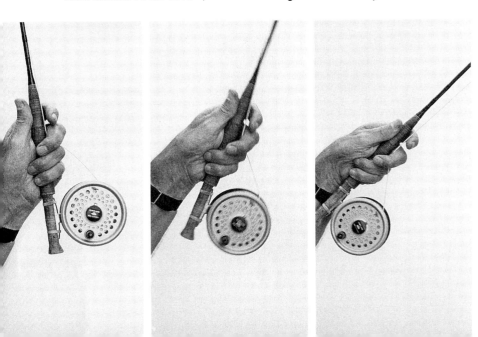

YOU'LL NOTICE THROUGHOUT THIS BOOK THAT WHEN I CAST, MY wrist will open out to the side on the backcast. Then I bring the wrist and the reel forward straight as I make the forward drift. I'm turning the rod on its vertical axis to get the power part of the rod into play. *But I'm not tilting it out of the casting plane that I've established.* You can see a good example of this back on pages 121–122.

The cast has to be a personal thing to some extent. Once you've incorporated the basic principles into your muscle-memory you of course will develop variations, idiocyncrasies, of your own—but never stray from the basics.

Speaking of rods, I prefer graphite. The thing about bamboo is you get deeper shock waves in your line off the rod tip on the backcast, so you have to drift the rod a little further forward before you make the forward stroke. Graphite's much more forgiving; the shock waves on your backcast from graphite are very shallow. You can apply a shorter stroke on the forward cast to get the job done with graphite.

The other thing about bamboo is, as you may imagine I'm hard on a rod. I respect the fine workmanship that goes into a good bamboo rod, however. Sometimes I'll fish a bamboo rod just for the sheer joy and beauty of it, the recreational aspect.

Temperature and Conditioning

YOU'VE GOT TO HAVE THE CAST, THE LEADER-AND-TIPPET COMBINA-tion, and the correct approach—look for the velocity changes, sun at your back (if possible), figure your cast out before you make it, avoid as many current changes as possible. But water-temperature—and conditioning—meaning what has the ongoing situation been—can't be emphasized enough.

Trout react to a variety of stimuli, but their basic metabolism is the key. It works this way: Trout need a balance of temperature and oxygen. As temperatures increase from 32 degrees to a range of 55 to 65 degrees, their metabolism accelerates and their body tissues demand more food.

Unless the water is polluted, the oxygen content is prime between 9 and 11 PPM. If the temperature continues to rise, the oxygen dissipates. Take the temperature to 70 degrees and feeding slows and migration starts. Trout move to colder waters. Increase the temperature to 80 degrees and, unless there is ample oxygen, the trout literally suffocate. In the spring, after an extended period of cold, if there is a sudden rise in water temperature and it becomes unseasonably warm for a period of about two weeks, the sudden increase in the trout's metabolism can end in starvation for the fish. Their body tissues desperately need nourishment. It's not forthcoming; the food chain isn't cooperating. This phenomenon can result in a fish kill.

But if there is enough oxygen, and trout are trapped, they can become conditioned to 70-degree-plus temperatures. I once did a clinic on a private stream near Philadelphia, Pennsylvania. The water temp was 78 degrees. The fish had nowhere to go; they were trapped. Rainbow trout were feeding on the surface, though the browns in the stream were in stress.

On the Yellow Breeches at the Allenberry Resort, Ed Shenk and I do several clinics a year. In mid-summer during hot spells the water temperatures can be 72 to 74 degrees across the stream, from one bank to the other. Fish can be caught, but the rainbows are more active than the browns; most browns taken are well under the vegetation in the shade. Cooler air temperatures in the morning and evening will move more fish, but the fact remains that fish can be caught at 74 degrees. These fish condition to these temperatures over a period of time.

Cold water is the other extreme. Immediately below the Navajo Dam in New Mexico the water temperatures are a constant 37 degrees. Only rainbows are found there. Brown trout are nonexistent. Rainbows feed readily at those temperatures. Those fish are conditioned to the cold waters. A few miles downstream, brown trout begin to appear in 50-degree-plus temperatures, and fishing is excellent for both species until air temperatures drop (morning and evening). Then they're tough to take. I tried night fishing when temperatures dropped from the 50s to the 40s and took a beating for one solid week from dark till 4:00 A.M.

Avalanche Lake in Glacier National Park is fed by snow run-off. Water temperatures seldom rise above 45 degrees in mid-summer; yet the cutthroats that inhabit the lake feed readily on top and just under the surface—and they're active. One afternoon where an ice water tributary entered the lake, the local trout population went crazy over a brace of wet flies. I managed two doubles. It's acclimation; it's conditioning.

Brook trout are active in colder temperatures. In April, when air and water temperatures are chilled—possibly not even reaching 50 degrees—brookies might be the only catchable fish. George Harvey, on a frigid first day on his favorite limestone stream in Pennsylvania (predominantly brown trout waters), could take only brook trout.

In early season, with high, cold waters, I'll move to smaller mountain streams where there is less water to cover—as in the smaller tribs—and trout are more active; rather than work the big water in the valley below in flood stage, where finding fish in all that water can be a problem and the native brown trout population can have a case of lockjaw.

Water chemistry, alkalinity, and ph have a great deal to do with finding fish and catching them. In normal conditions in a healthy environment, the ph may be 7; drop it to 4 and the stream becomes too acidic for survival unless a conditioning process has been ongoing. Studies and research by Swarts, Dunson, and Wright, with the assistance of William Kennedy of the Pennsylvania Fish Commission, found that native brook trout and certain strains of brook trout could withstand a lower ph. Through acclimation, trout conditioned to acid

waters. A resistance was built up and through selective spawning of resistant genetic strains, from the embryo state to the swim-up fry (in low ph environs—4.4 to 4.7), resistance to acid conditions was enhanced.

Another study by Joe O'Grodnick, Pennsylvania fisheries biologist, found that certain strains of brook trout could withstand a ph factor as low as 4.4.

Each year I fish a mountain stream that drains a bog. Several miles downstream I catch native brookies and browns, the browns being the predominant species. Closer to the bog, the stream contains only brookies; within the bog and immediately below, there are no fish. Understanding the ph and conditioning factor not only tells me where to fish, but for what species.

Stocked trout are conditioned daily to overhead feeding. From the time they lose their egg sacks till they're stocked, they are fed overhead. Once they're stocked, artificial feeding stops, but they're still looking for food in the upper level. I've taken stocked trout of all three strains—brook, brown, and rainbows—early in the season in water temperatures between 40 and 50 degrees with wet flies just under the surface.

Once trout are conditioned to temperatures in the optimum range of 55 to 65 degrees and there is a sudden and dramatic change to lower temperatures, they can cut off.

George Harvey and I were on a Pennsylvania limestone stream one morning after a cold spell had hit the night before. The stream temperatures dropped to 50 degrees after being in the high 50s. A couple of days before, I had had good luck on a Hendrickson hatch and expected more of the same. George's comment after he took a temperature reading was, ''We'll not take a fish this morning.'' He was right. We didn't.

Pay attention to where spring sources come in. You can have as much as a 10-degree drop in temperature. If it's a sizable spring, a considerable distance below that spring trout will hug the bank on that same side. You don't want to get too far below the source if that source is not great. Intermixing of the parent stream with the spring flow brings the temperatures up rapidly as you get

. . . if you see white sand or white sand and gravel . . . you probably have a spring . . .

downstream of that source. The amount of spring water coming in is very important to where you make your approach. In most cases you can see the difference in water clarity where that spring water's coming in.

Let's say you're in a place where there's a cold spring coming in, say on big Pine Creek in Pennsylvania. If you have a cold spring coming off the bottom or a cold trib coming in, you may get a 5-degree change, possibly a 10-degree change if the cold trib is large enough.

Big Pine is 74. Cedar Run where it comes in, is 63—they intermix. Just a few feet below it's 68. Go downstream 40 feet or so and you're out of the productive area.

Another aspect of temperature is the deep hole. When that air temperature holds from say 72 to 78 for 4 to 8 hours those fish—it's like somebody rings a bell—start to migrate.

In the first stage they move into the deep holes. It's slightly cooler there, maybe a couple degrees cooler.

As an example: There's a 10-foot deep hole right below where Cedar Run is confluent with Pine. In my soundings there I've found that when the main stream is 74, it's 71 degrees at the bottom of that hole. So there's a 3-degree difference. You might get a 3- or a 4-degree difference in a deep hole. That's enough to hold trout in that first stage of the migration. The water has not really started to hold the higher temperatures for an extended period of time.

At such times fish early in the morning or fish late in the evening and at night. That's when you get your temperature changes and that's when they start to move. The cold air drops at night and holds until early morning. The fish move into the riff to feed where there is a greater amount of oxygen.

As the heat wave increases in intensity and the water's losing oxygen, the trout start the second stage of the migration. They head for the cold tribs and spring holes. They'll lay in the mouths of those tributaries coming in, and in the spring holes. If the water is low at the mouth of the trib, impeding migration, they'll wait until the first heavy rain. Then they move up. A good heavy rain will push them up into the tribs.

I've hit the mouths of tribs at night and done extremely well then come back a couple weeks later and caught fish, but not nearly as many. The population had gone on up the trib.

A student said to me one time in a class, "Well, you told me if I went up this tributary I'd catch fish because it's colder. So I went up the tributary and I didn't catch anything."

I asked, "Did you take a thermometer?"

"No," he said. What he didn't realize was that the bottom of that tributary was marginal. Some of the tribs can be marginal; they've been lumbered off, they have broad flood-plains, they're exposed.

So you take your thermometer and walk the trib, or you go above the cut-off point on the parent or main stream, where it starts to get colder as you go higher.

On any water I've never fished before, first thing I do is take a temperature reading. Before I'd even make a cast I'd take the temperature. If it was 72, or even 68 degrees by 10:00 A.M., I wouldn't fish. I'd walk. I'd look for a spring. I'd try to find a cold source. Now I might have to walk a distance or get in the car and drive. I'll go to the headwaters of that stream, if I have to, to find optimum temperature. When looking for colder tribs take a look at the topography. Look at the lay of the land. Look for the gaps and draws.

Here's a little experience I had. I was doing a clinic on the Lackawaxen, near Scranton, Pennsylvania, and in the morning I gave them a show on water temperature. I'd been told the Lackawaxen was a fantastic stream to fish and had a great trout population.

I go to the stream expecting wonderful things, expecting to have a chance to show some nymphing techniques and show these people the different ramifications thereof—I get out the thermometer and put it in the water. Talk about water temperatures! When I put my hand in that water it was like a bathtub. The water was 80 degrees.

I said, "There's no use—I can show you techniques but there's no use in me trying to catch a fish."

"Well," they said, "let's go where you can catch a fish."

I said, "Yeah, fine, where?"

I had talked about topography, where the draws are, where gaps are . . . the highway parallels the Lackawaxen. We started to drive. There were I-don't-know-how-many cars in that caravan. We're going down the road and all at once I see where the mountain drops, a gap. We pull over—I see a railroad bridge . . .

Right away I said, "There's a bridge. The bridge spans something."

So we donned our gear and waded across. Sure enough, here was a stream coming in. The stream was 68 degrees. Where it hit the mouth of the Lackawaxen it was about 72 degrees. And where that stream entered the Lackawaxen there must have been 400 trout. They were just jammed, all pushed with their noses right up to the cooler water—that was in July or August. They'd had an extended hot spell. So that was one case where the topography gave me the tip.

If you see watercress, that's an indicator. Look for colder water there. If you see duckweed, if you see white sand, or gravel on the bottom, you probably have a spring coming up there.

A big outcropping of stone—limestone or shale—look for your spring at the base of the outcropping.

Or you see that a cold trib that was coming in all spring has dried up suddenly . . . well, it probably didn't dry up at all. Walk upstream 50 yards and the stream is still flowing. The water goes underground and it comes out at the same place it always has, only now it's coming out underneath, under the

surface of the parent stream—it's a cold seep now, and it pulls those trout right to it, same as before . . .

You have to consider not only the temperature but the conditioning—the context . . . I said I wouldn't even fish if I got a reading of 72, but that's in a situation where the whole stream had heated to 72. What about my experience on the Lackawaxen? There I found *80 degree* water, so when I got in my car and found that trib coming in at 68, the 72-degree reading where the two mixed represented *cooler* water and oxygen for those trout—and there they were, not feeding but existing. There was enough oxygen for survival. Now at least I knew where the fish were. I might have taken some that night.

Spring morning on a Pennsylvania limestone stream. That sulphur's going to start coming off soon but it's still chilly, not much is happening, they're underneath. The sulphur nymph's not moving yet. So you sit down on the bank and wait 'til the temperature gets higher? No. You consider the conditioning aspect. What have those fish been feeding on all year long? What's the mainstay of the food chain that's coming to them year 'round? The answer here is the cress bug, and if you didn't happen to know that, a close examination of some stream vegetation or the bottom of a stone might give you a good idea. So you fish the cress bug, and you pick up some nice fish—then as the air warms the water the sulphurs start to pop. Nymphal and hatching activity triggers the trout to go to the sulphur, so you switch. In mid and late spring, mayfly hatches prompt surface feeding. It's the beginning of a conditioning process. Trout begin to look up for part of their food supply. The conditioning continues on into the summer as terrestrial insects, ants, beetles, crickets, and inchworms floating on the surface become important. Trout condition to surface-feed.

You can't isolate. You can't put strict laws and guidelines down about the way trout are going to act. There've been some recent studies done, and they have value, but you can't generalize from them—the people who did those studies were watching trout that first of all weren't fished over, and second that were in one specific location on the stream . . . you have to be aware of what trout do in a multitude of different stream situations, and if you're an angler you're interested in how trout that are regularly fished over behave. Some studies say trout don't necessarily hide, the big ones will come out to feed in broad daylight; they don't necessarily shun light. There may be isolated bits of truth in these conclusions reached about trout that have never been subjected to heavy fishing pressure, but the norm of behavior I'm interested in as a fly-fisherman relates to the behavior of trout that are conditioned to man.

Trout condition not only to temperature, but to the size, shape, color, and motion of an insect—and the predominance of them. They locate where food is most readily intercepted. They condition to the food chain in every aspect.

Fishing a sulphur hatch one evening, I was being completely shut out. A half-dozen trout were rising directly in front of me. Frustrated, I waded to the bank and sat down to assess the situation. Darkness settled in and the trout were still feeding. I flashed my flex light on the water. There, trapped within the fine mesh of my landing net, were small sulphurs. My fly had been two sizes too big. I found a #18, attached it to my leader, waded into position, and caught three of those fish. Not only were those fish conditioned to size but they inhaled those small flies in total darkness! Size can make a difference both in daylight and darkness. Don't think trout can't see after dark. They have excellent eyesight on top and underneath.

I can't count the number of times in my youthful early experiences when I would cast my arm off to no avail over trout sipping and slashing caddis flies on the surface—simply because I didn't understand how important shape and silhouette can be. The upright float of a dry fly just didn't do it—they wanted the flat tent-wing image. They were conditioned to shape and silhouette—and movement.

One night on a big limestone stream the Greek Drake hatch was in full swing. I was fishless after an hour, with four good fish rising in front of me and in close to the bank. I crawled on my stomach to within a few feet of those fish and witnessed that only the flies that moved were intercepted. Dead, drifting flies were ignored. Movement can be a conditioner.

I feel strongly that, though upright wings may not be visible to the trout, air currents on the surface of the water impart movement to the fly as well as the interplay of water currents on good, stiff, well-proportioned (equal distribution around the hook) hackles. That bouncing, rocking, side-to-side motion entices trout. I've watched this phenomenon too many times to dispute it.

Shape, silhouette, and movement all can figure in the conditioning process. Several years ago I began undersizing the hackles on spinner ties to achieve two effects, a flat-profile float and movement in response to water and air currents. (Use three undersized, one-half-the-gap stiff hackles.) This particular tie has been very successful for me.

The intensity of the hatch and the amount of insects both underwater and on top are other important conditioning factors. Nymphal action as a hatch gets underway triggers bottom feeding. As the hatch progresses and insects begin to pop to the surface, the greater insect population still remains down. Though trout may rise to intercept nymphs, the action is under the surface.

So many times when flyfishermen see a few fish break on the surface, it's the fishermen that become conditioned to those few fish, though the bulk of the fish population remains down. Then, there is that moment when the majority of the trout will surface-feed. When the duns and spinners fill the air and the predominance of the hatch is top-side, the fish condition to numbers. (But not all the fish. Often the monster trout chomp on some helpless fish that is in a feeding frenzy and has let its guard down.) Just as trout condition to nymphal activity on the bottom in colder waters and throughout hatching activity within the year, they also condition to the food supply and, later in the summer months, that can be on top.

On most streams in the country, but particularly on the eastern freestone streams, the ant, beetle, cricket, and other terrestrial insects become the bulk of the fish's diet. The fish condition to surface activity, and on many limestone streams the Trico hatch starts in July and lasts into September and even October. They stimulate the trout to move on top in the morning then switch to terrestrials on top in the afternoon. The fish are looking up for their food—it's a conditioning process.

The greatest problem the fisherman has is knowing what specific insects the fish have conditioned to. This happens often in late spring when there are numerous hatches occurring at the same time or within a time span when one hatch is dominant. I've seen flyfishers throw their arms off on a Green Drake hatch, which seemed the obvious selection, when the trout were feeding on small sulphurs.

Trout become conditioned to light intensity or the lack of it. I enjoy fishing for brown trout after dark. For years I've watched streams come alive after the light went out. Fish that are never seen in daylight hours materialize as if by magic when darkness has descended. I realize temperatures can be a factor here. In the summer months when darkness falls, cooler night air intermixes with water to lower temperatures and increase oxygen. But I've taken enough browns in the late fall and on winter nights to know that it's the lack of light that stirs the fish.

The silhouette, the profile, of a fly on the surface can be an important factor. A down-wing imitation on a caddis hatch, or a low-profile float of a spent spinner, can be the answer . . . and maybe the only one. (Left to right) 1) a spent-wing sulphur spinner, three undersized hackles ½ the hook gap; 2) a down-wing caddis; 3) a parachute green drake; 4) a skater; 5) a hair-wing stonefly; 6) a three-hackle sulphur with an upright wing.

Pass Something On

I WAS TRYING TO LEARN TO DISTANCE-CAST IN THE BRUSH. IT WAS late in the season and the water was low and clear. My casting stroke was far too long, I didn't have the knowledge and I didn't have the control. I was spooking every fish I cast to. No matter what I did, instead of my fly shooting in under that low-hanging branch it hung over it, my leader opened up and looped over the branch . . . I was young, I was cocky, and I didn't know what the hell I was doing. I kept casting and I kept getting hung up and the harder I tried the worse it got and the more frustrated I became until finally I was crazy. I was so upset with myself I turned around and thrashed my rod on the ground in total frustration until it splintered.

I was damn near in tears.

But I went back, I went back and kept trying until I figured it out. I was determined to figure out how to cast for distance in the brush and under those trees, and at last I did. I learned to shorten that stroke—use just wrist and thumb. I learned to adjust the leader for the conditions I was facing. I worked and I experimented and I never gave up until I had the knowledge and skills I needed—but you can't do it alone.

I was lucky when I was young. George Harvey was my flyfishing idol, and

from childhood through my formative years of college he was helping to shape my future, though I was unaware of it at the time. In 1970 when George was preparing for retirement from Penn State University, where he taught an estimated 36,000 students to flyfish, he arranged for me to take his place as head of the angling program. George took me under his wing and took the trouble to pass on to me his vast knowledge. So much of what I know comes from George. Some of it I've been able to expand on and experiment with, developing my own techniques and strategies. But George is my mentor and, as I say, I've been just incredibly lucky.

I owe George and I'll never be able to repay him, but what I can do is I can try to teach others. That's the way you pay it all back. You pass it on. It's as important as catching fish.